By What
Authority?

Mark P. Shea

By What Authority?

An Evangelical Discovers ✝ Catholic Tradition

Our Sunday Visitor Publishing Division
Our Sunday Visitor, Inc.
Huntington, Indiana 46750

ISBN: 0-87973-851-0
LCCCN: 96-68288

Cover design by: Monica Watts

Printed in the United States of America
851

Dedication

to Father Michael Sweeney, O.P.

Father and Friend

CONTENTS

Acknowledgments

This book is a product of collaboration with persons whose consciousness of their collaboration ranged from "blank unawareness" to "omniscience." On the "omniscience" end of the scale I would like to cheerfully put my Lord and God, the Father, Son, and Holy Spirit, from whom, to whom, and through whom this book and all things exist. Blessed be he!

A little lower down the scale I would like to place my beloved Janet, whose enormous patience with and support of this project has made the impossible possible. Likewise, I want to thank our boys, Luke and Matthew, for sharing the computer with Dad.

Slightly less omniscient than my wife is the editorial Whiz Kid Sherry Weddell, whose typically incisive comments were as valuable as her steady stream of research resources. Thanks once again!

Also big on the editorial acumen scale are Sherry Curp, whose efficiency and compassion are no risk, and the following profoundly helpful and inspirational people who are listed, not according to omniscience but according to alphabet:

James Akin: for help and support, both technical and personal, I offer sincere thanks.

J.S. Bach: who piped music into my stereo straight from heaven during the long months of writing.

The people of the Blessed Sacrament parish in Seattle, Washington: what a blessing and a sacrament you are!

G.K. Chesterton: my hero.

Richard Aquinas Chonak: tracker-downer of obscure hymnists.

Cat Clark: Research Maven Who Must Be Obeyed. You made an invaluable contribution to this project, Cat. Thanks a million!

Dave Curp: Historian Extraordinaire and Beloved Brother.

Mike Drollman: Strategic Prayer Support Reservist.

Greg Erlandson: for his wonderful generosity and support.

James Felak: Graduate Advisor to Historians Extraordinaire and Beloved Brother.

The Greenlake Christian Institute: tough-minded Protestants and splendid brothers and sisters in Christ.

Gospel Life Church: my first home in Christ.

Marcus Grodi: many thanks for your interest and support.

Steven Greydanus: Arthurian author, artist, and dear friend.

Scott Hahn: who is for Catholic apologetics what Randy Johnson is for the Seattle Mariners. Thanks for working to foster Big Unity in the Body of Christ.

Martin Helgesen: Researcher Extraordinaire and Grand Poobah of Radio Free Thulcandra, from whom I shamelessly stole material for the appendix. Great gobs of temporal thanks.

John and Sue Jensen: dear friends in the communion of saints (whom only distance separates from my heart).

Luke Timothy Johnson: fight the good fight.

Brad Kaiser: Cyber.friend and Golden Skewer of Orthodoxy.

Karl Keating: thanks bunches for healing financial hemorrhages.

Peter Kreeft: another of my heroes.

Bill Lewis: Retsina Lover, Twenty-percent Calvinist, and Biking Buddy.

C.S. Lewis: yet another of my heroes.

The Nameless Lay Group: Catholic laity blending love, orthodoxy, and spunk!

Lou Nunez: Jolly Joisey Jesuit, Handy Biblical Reference Guy, and Mariners Fan.

Scott Anthony McKellar: Gentleman and Scholar.

Dan O'Neill: much obliged for guidance through the Dark Wood of my ignorance.

The Seattle Great Books Reading Group: more fun than three other reading groups.

Father Peter Stravinskas: may God prosper the work of your hands.

John Michael Talbot: deep gratitude for your work in the Great Regathering.

Dale Vree: who lets me make house calls on the *New Oxford Review* and who has enthusiastically supported this project and this writer far beyond my worth.

Steve Wood: profound gratitude for your enthusiastic support!

A special vote of thanks to Jim Manney, editor and all-around good guy. Thanks for going to bat for this book.

Also special thanks to saints Athanasius, Anthony of the Desert, and Francis de Sales, on whose constant intercession I relied for help. *Ora pro nobis.*

And, at the "blank unawareness" end of the spectrum, I want to thank Peter Christopher Shea, who was born while this book was being written, and who breathed softly in the crib next to the computer many nights while I burned the midnight oil. In its own sweet way, little one, such breath has been my dearest inspiration. Thanks be to God for his indescribable gift!

PREFACE

As the editor of a nearly ten-year-old periodical dedicated to apologetics, I come across hundreds of articles from budding authors who think they are proposing something unique. And some do. One such writer was Mark Shea, who first submitted items for consideration a number of years back. Several things struck me about this convert-writer's content and style. First, the subject matter was good and accurately presented; second, the mode of communication was fresh and vibrant; third, the author wrote from a perspective of faith, as well as from interesting, generally unexplored angles. This combination of factors has ensured that Mark would grace the pages of *The Catholic Answer* on many occasions.

When I heard that Mark had produced a book, I was pleased because I knew that all of the assets cited above would be in evidence in a full-blown study. When I discovered that his topic was "Tradition," I was thoroughly delighted. Why? Because of all the neuralgic issues in apologetics and in ecumenical dialogue alike, no subject is more fundamental than that of Tradition.

Now, truth be told, there is no shortage of works on Tradition, so why another one? Because Mark has a marvelous way of "backing into" a sensitive topic. In this volume, he handles the formal study deftly by a most useful inductive methodology; what is particularly helpful is the autobiographical nature of his discovery of Tradition and its central role in Christian faith, revelation, and theology. Our author, you see, attempts to handle this crucial theme by appealing to "head" and "heart" at one and the same time. As an academic, as a writer, and as a pastor, I feel compelled to assert that he succeeds admirably.

"Cradle Catholics," Evangelicals, and various other honest seekers will all find something of value and interest here. And they should enjoy themselves in the process as Mark Shea demonstrates that Tradition is no dead, desiccated fossil but the very lifeblood of Christianity. G. K. Chesterton, another convert and lay apologist of this century, once warned of how simple, basic things can become convoluted:

> Step softly, under snow or rain,
> To find the place where men can pray;
> The way is all so very plain
> That we may lose the way (*The Wise Men*).

Mark Shea offers us a road map which puts and keeps all in focus, so that Catholics would not "lose the way" and others would be able to find it. He is an excellent tour guide because he has made the trip himself; he knows, both intellectually and affectively, the roadblocks and the shortcuts. I pray that you will appreciate this journey into the land of Tradition.

Rev. Peter M.J. Stravinskas, Ph.D., STD
Editor, *The Catholic Answer*

FOREWORD

Just a year or so before his much-publicized conversion, Tom Howard expressed his own growing sense of Protestant inadequacy in a work aptly entitled, *Evangelical Is Not Enough*. Mark Shea's new book, *By What Authority?* —though clearly not intended as a sequel — delivers the positive follow-up message: Evangelical and Catholic ARE enough.

I suspect that different readers may react very differently to that last statement. On the one hand, a stalwart Protestant may take it to be an oxymoron ("Evangelical Catholics are like married bachelors"). On the other hand, a traditionalist Catholic may be wondering why "Evangelical" is even needed ("Catholic is enough by itself").

In this luminous treatment of religious authority, Mark Shea shows how both terms actually imply each other. Thus, to be fully consistent with Scripture, an Evangelical will become a Catholic; just as a faithful adherence to Catholic tradition calls for a truly Evangelical commitment and witness. As a reader, I guarantee that you will be challenged by such a balanced yet forceful approach ("Evangelical and Catholic — both or neither").

There are other qualities in this book that make it special. For one thing, Shea writes with considerable skill and wit. From start to finish, reading this book is a breeze. Given the tough and profound issues that Shea treats, plus the degree of difficulty in debating them fairly, attentive readers will gratefully give his writing style some very high scores.

Another strength of the book is its timeliness, especially in view of the much publicized Jesus Seminar, whose members (Crossan, Funk, etc.) have all become media sensations by employing a fundamentalist style of liberal exegesis (call it "hysterical criticism") in order to reject as inauthentic the vast majority of sayings attributed to Jesus by the evangelists — to which Shea responds with gentle yet forceful persuasion. But the thing I like most about this book is the crystal clear and compelling case that Shea makes — on the basis of logic, history, and Scripture — for sacred ("big T") Tradition. It is simply the best that I have found.

Read this book carefully. And keep a pen and notepad nearby. I guarantee rich dividends for your investment of time and energy.

Scott Hahn
Associate Professor of Theology
Franciscan University of Steubenville

OF KICKING LADDERS
AND COUNTING RINGS
AN APPRECIATION OF MY
EVANGELICAL HERITAGE

*If I forget you, O Jerusalem, may my right hand
forget its skill! — Ps 137:5*

This is a book about a change of heart and mind. Specifically, it is a book about how an Evangelical who believed the Holy Scriptures to be the sole source of the Christian revelation came to discover and embrace the ancient Catholic teaching that Sacred Tradition is a source of revelation too. It is written for those Catholics who wish to find a way to speak of the Faith to their Evangelical brothers and sisters that is not alienating but intelligible. It is written for Catholics who wish to understand more clearly the very real impediments to faith an Evangelical often encounters when he or she thinks of the Catholic Faith. Further, it written for the Evangelical who wishes to confront that Faith and, in particular, its claim that the gospel is not fully expressed apart from Sacred Tradition. And it is written for those, both Catholic and Evangelical, who seek to know how to speak to one another of their faith in our Lord Jesus Christ and come to a closer unity and love in the Holy Spirit, as our Lord commands us.

But before we can get to where this book is going, it is vital (especially if one really takes Tradition seriously) to know where its author has been. In the case of this particular book, this is true for two reasons.

First, this book is an attempt to chart the course of a long journey which occurred in my soul. To do this, I had two options. I could tell the story in the chronological order of events, hoping the reader would be able to make sense of the sprawling mess of intuitive leaps, backtracking, sudden storms of doubt, blank confusion, false leads, tedious hours of study, lucky breaks, prayer, and happenstance conversations that went into the turbulent process of thinking this issue through. The problem with this approach is that it leaves the reader as confused in *reading* about my journey as I was in *living* it.

Therefore, as St. Papias said of a far greater Mark, this author opted instead to "write down accurately whatever he remembered, though not in order" or, at any rate, not in chronological order. The resulting narrative has, I hope, much clearer lines while still remaining true to the fact that every single one of the questions addressed here are questions which I wrestled with at some point in my journey.

The second reason it is important to know where the author has been is because our culture is thoroughly dominated by the notion that "change" equals "repudiation of the past." Thus, not only is everyone from movie stars to political figures forever going through "phases," but even in the Church we find people who assume that to change means to reject the past. That is why the Christian world is awash in conversion stories, the accepted formula of which is:

1. I used to be one of those X's.
2. Then I found out that:
    a. Y's were all right, and
    b. X's were all wrong.
3. Thank God I'm not an X anymore.

In short, the common picture of change in the modern (particularly American) world, both secular and religious, is of a man climbing a series of intellectual ladders and kicking each one down in scorn after he has reached some new plane of spiritual or intellectual growth. Everything that got him to where he is now is outdated and — mark this — therefore false.

Don't misunderstand. I believe in the biblical demand for repentance and a decisive turning away from evil. But this is not what we are talking about here. Rather we are talking about a typically modern mind-set that tends to identify "previous" with "bad, disproved, ridiculous, and rejected." It is this mind-set I wish, paradoxically enough, to reject at the outset. I emphatically do *not* think it necessary or desirable to repudiate my Evangelical roots in order to embrace Sacred Tradition. Indeed, the Tradition I have come to regard as revelatory positively insists that God's grace builds on, rather than repudiates, the good things in God's good world — including the great good thing called Evangelicalism. Thus, just as the New Testament praises the Old, just as St. Paul praises his native Judaism (Rom 3:1-2), just as Christ fulfills rather than annihilates his Jewish roots (Mt 5:17), so I believe Catholic Tradition builds on all I received from Evangelicalism.

So before we talk about why I came to believe in the truth of Sacred Tradition, I believe it essential to count the core Evangelical growth rings on the tree of my Christian life and praise God for the good wood he gave me in my years as a Protestant. Indeed, if what follows is to make sense, it can only do so in light of what God gave me through the first Christian community to which Christ called me after a life of fuzzy agnosticism. That community was Protestant Evangelicalism. It was largely through Evangelicalism that I became a believer in Jesus Christ at the age of twenty. Likewise it was largely through Evangelicalism that the Holy Spirit laid all the groundwork for me to see and embrace Sacred Tradition as revelation. Therefore, it is to these fine Christian people that I owe an unpayable debt of gratitude for the following reasons:

First and foremost, it was Evangelicals who showed me how to look to Jesus Christ as the source of salvation. As I learned my faith from them, I learned that it is nonsense (and a terrible burden) to imagine I have to earn the free grace of God. Instead, they taught me that God has already done the work of forgiving my sin and making a way for me to approach him through the Cross of Jesus Christ. This is, of course, a basic message of Scripture. But without the continual reminder of my Evangelical brothers and sisters, this truth was tough to hold on to at first. So I am grateful that, by both word and deed, they drilled it into me till it stuck.

Second, they taught me to reverence Scripture in a practical, living way. Under their tutelage I experienced Scripture as the living word of God for the first time. Because of them, I learned to study Scripture and to work through its sometimes baffling mysteries with patience and prayer. By their wisdom, I was rescued from numerous errors in understanding it. As charismatics who believed in the reality of the Spirit's voice, they never lost sight of the fact that he can never contradict the Scriptures. On their lips I heard the Scriptures come to life, alloyed with real prayers and deeds done in power and effective to enact the will of God by the Holy Spirit.

Third, it was from Evangelicals that I learned believing, effective prayer. They showed me that prayer is the first, not the last, resort. "Pray first, then act" was the great principle I learned from Evangelicalism. "Seek first the Kingdom," as our Lord says. After that logistics and resource acquisition get easier.

But far greater than learning to trust God in "request prayer" was the Evangelical instinct to zero in on "worship prayer" whether or not God ever granted a request. "Praise God!" was the great Evangelical exclamation I learned, an exclamation that marvelously sums up all of Evangelicalism. And I learned that this exclamation was not some empty religious phrase uttered by televangelists, but a sign of Evangelicalism's willed (and sometimes heroic) choice to say, with Job, "Though he slay me, yet will I hope in him" (Job 13:15).

For I have seen my Evangelical brothers and sisters offer prayers of praise to God in the depths of agony. Not long ago I attended a funeral for a friend's wife who had died suddenly.

They had been married four short years. She was not yet thirty. Her husband loved her as much as any man has ever loved a woman. Yet the funeral was, by his choice, an act of praise to God first and only secondly an expression of his wrenching grief. The courage and glory of it still grips my heart. It was as brave and devout an act as any ancient martyr's prayer. But it does not surprise me, for I saw many such examples among Evangelicals of trust in him who went through death for us. And by such examples I learned that prayer, though it involves request, must first involve adoration of God for who he is, and not for what he might do for me in this life. For he has already done everything by going to the terrible death of Golgotha and winning a place for me (and my friend's wife and all the rest of us) at his Father's right hand. May God be praised for his many Evangelical saints who bear witness to this with the courage and integrity of my friend.

Such integrity was what taught me a fourth blessing in Christ: how to live my faith in community. Which is to say, it taught me how to live in the Spirit of Christ rather than trust in my own self-defensiveness and personal resources. For these were people who passionately believed in the reality of the supernatural life and taught me to recognize that, without the present grace of Christ supporting and sustaining our every breath, there was *nothing* we could do. They had nothing to do with either self-ishness or with its flip side, religious do-goodism. They rejected both as equal and opposite forms of godless self-sufficiency — mere schemes to earn brownie points with either God or man. They were equally impatient with works righteousness (which they thought Catholics believed in) and the social gospel of some mainline Protestant churches which reduces the Faith to politically correct involvement in the League of Women Voters. For my Evangelical brothers and sisters, everything had to be rooted in Christ and aimed at union with him or it was regarded with suspicion as mere secular humanism.

Yet such a rejection of humanistic self-sufficiency did not mean a rejection of responsibility. For, in Christ, these people were a dynamo of loving service to their neighbors. This included pooling their money to help financially strapped members of the church, organizing youth ministries, organizing music ministries, helping struggling families get on their feet, working in pro-life activities, assisting college students, sponsoring Romanian, Polish, and Vietnamese immigrants into the United States (taking them into their homes till they could get on their feet), and ardently pursuing various evangelistic endeavors. For a number of new Americans, it was my old church that was Christ incarnate to them when they first arrived on American shores destitute, jobless, and unable to speak a word of English. May they never lose their reward for the good they did these people.

And may they be remembered for teaching me responsibility as well. For it was my Evangelical family in Christ who taught me how to shoulder my duties in the Lord and honestly confess my sins. They showed me by example how to quit making excuses and admit failure frankly. They showed me endless gobs of mercy and patience as I flailed about in ignorance and selfishness. They saved my bacon times without number when my faith weakened or got swamped by doubts. They prayed for me to become a believer when I was skulking on the fringes of agnosticism and fancying myself superior to "those religious types." They rejoiced over me when I at last made my submission to Jesus. They taught me not to shy away from truth even when it was scary. They taught me both to bend my knee like the sinner I am and lift up my head with the dignity of Christ.

But best of all, Evangelicals taught me to never be satisfied if God desires to give more. Just as the Israelites followed the pillar of cloud and the pillar of fire, so my Evangelical mentors in Christ were ardent about pursuing truth wherever it might lead. They frequently reminded me of the wisdom of Paul: "Test everything. Hold on to the good" (1 Th 5:21). From them I learned that the Christian life is nothing if not adventurous and willing to mine all of experience for those nuggets of truth God has hidden in the world. As my old pastor used to quote Proverbs 25:2, "It is the glory of God to conceal a matter; to search out a matter is the glory of kings." For they knew that no truth could ever conflict with the God of truth and every true thing could only make a disciple into a better disciple.

It is this last point which is the launch pad for what follows. For paradoxically, it was my struggle to defend the faith as Evangelical Christianity taught it that helped me see the Faith as Catholic Christianity teaches it, a Faith revealed not only by the Bible but by Sacred Tradition as well. It was my Evangelical love of Scripture that led to my Catholic love of Sacred Tradition. It was the solid Bible preaching of Evangelicalism that built the foundation in my mind and heart for the solid teaching of the Catholic Faith. And it is the Catholic Faith, revealed by both Scripture and Tradition, that is helping me fulfill the consuming desire of my Evangelical heritage: to be a faithful disciple and witness of Jesus Christ.

It is then out of gratitude for and obedience to my Evangelical and Catholic family in Christ that I bear such meager witness as I can to Sacred Tradition: gratitude for the heart cry of adoration taught me by my Evangelical family of faith and obedience to their steadfast commitment to truth, a commitment which has grown like the mustard seed into a love of the Catholic Tradition. And most of all, I offer this work to the honor and glory of God the Father, Son, and Holy Spirit, so steadfastly served by my Catholic and Evangelical families, in the hope that by his creative, loving and unifying hand we may all, in the words of Paul, "reach unity in the faith and in the knowledge of the Son of God" (Eph 4:13).

CHAPTER ONE
THE TRADITIONS
OF MEN

*Though St. John the Evangelist saw many strange monsters
in his vision, he saw no creature so wild as one of his
own commentators. — G.K. Chesterton*

When I was an Evangelical Protestant, I frequently bumped into Catholics who made bold to venture a belief in purgatory or offer a prayer to a saint. When they did so, I got puzzled. Especially since the people who held these sorts of beliefs almost invariably couldn't give me any biblical proof of them. Didn't they believe the Bible? Yet the Bible doesn't mention purgatory. It nowhere urges us to "Pray to saints." Quite the opposite, I said, it teaches that there is no second chance for us after death[1] and that there is, not a bunch of saints, but "one mediator between God and men, the man Christ Jesus" (1 Tm 2:5). So why did these Catholics encumber themselves with all this baroque encrustation of tradition instead of just sticking to the simple word of God? Especially since that word spoke very loudly about tradition:

It said, "Beware of the leaven of the Pharisees" (Mk 8:15 RSV).

For that, after all, is why Jesus warned in no uncertain terms about human tradition. He rebuked the Pharisees roundly, asking, "Why do you break the command of God for the sake of your tradition?" (Mt 15:3). He berated them, saying, "You nullify the word of God for the sake of your tradition" (Mt 15:6). He declared, "You have let go of the commands of God and are holding on to the traditions of men" (Mk 7:8). He applied the dire prophecy of Scripture to them with the terrible verdict: "They worship me in vain; their teachings are but rules taught by men" (Mk 7:7).

Nor were these warnings lost on the apostles. For throughout Scripture, we find them carrying on this hue and cry against allowing human tradition to fidget with and supplant God's revelation. Paul, for instance, cautions the Colossians against buying into "hollow and deceptive philosophy, which depends on human tradition and the basic principles of this world rather than on Christ" (Col 2:8). Peter also warns of the empty way of life "received by tradition from your fathers" (1 Pt 1:18 KJV). Darker still, Paul prophesies that the day will surely come when "some will abandon the faith and follow deceiving spirits and things taught by demons" (1 Tm 4:1). Luke also records Paul's warning to the Ephesian elders that "after I leave, savage wolves will come in among you and will not spare the flock. Even from your own number men will arise and distort the truth in order to draw away disciples after them" (Acts 20:29-30).

So I took a dim view of the traditions of men. Especially because, as I surveyed the contemporary scene, it didn't take a rocket scientist to see human tradition springing up everywhere with a brazenness that almost evokes a kind of perverse admiration for the con artists who get away with it.

Consider, for example, the latest cutting-edge offerings from Episcopal Bishop John Shelby Spong. Bishop Spong is the author of such works as *Born of a Woman: A Bishop Rethinks the Birth of Jesus*; *Rescuing the Bible from Fundamentalism: A Bishop Rethinks the Meaning of Scripture;* and his most recent effort *Resurrection: Myth or Reality?* In Dr. Spong's lexicon, "rethinks" appears to be synonymous with "explains away" or "radically cheapens," while "Fundamentalism" appears to be synonymous with "Anything that looks remotely like it takes Scripture as the authoritative and revealed word of God."

Dr. Spong "rethinks" many things. Thus, in his last book, he unveils his startling discovery that, because Paul was aware of his sinfulness, the apostle was in all likelihood a repressed homosexual:

> Paul felt tremendous guilt and shame, which produced in him self-loathing. The presence of homosexuality would have created this response among Jewish people in that period of history. Nothing else, in my opinion, could account for Paul's self-judging rhetoric, his negative feeling toward his own body, and his sense of being controlled by something he had no power to change. . . . Nothing else accounts for this data as well as the possibility that Paul was a gay male.[2]

Then, in his next book, Bishop Spong builds on this solid exegetical legacy by declaring, "I do not believe that Mary was in any biological sense literally a virgin."[3] How does he account for the birth of Christ? With the novel insight that the Virgin Mary was probably a rape victim:

> Was [Jesus'] origin more scandalous than the violation of a betrothal relationship? Was it so scandalous in fact that it could be countered only by the creation of a supernatural birth tradition? Was Jesus the child of adultery, the product of seduction? Was Mary a violated woman, the victim of rape? . . . Could the Holy Spirit be perceived as validating a child conceived in either rape or seduction as a life chosen by

> God for the accomplishment of God's will?
> . . . Is it possible that Mary was a violated
> person and that people referred to her as
> "the virgin" who had been raped so that
> Mary the Virgin became the way people
> thought of her and the name by which they
> called her? . . . Only an illegitimate preg-
> nancy could make sense out of that desig-
> nation ["lowly" in the Magnificat], and
> only an illegitimate child and its mother
> who were fully incorporated into Israel
> could sing of future generations who would
> call a humiliated woman blessed . . . .[4]

After that, more insights pour forth, ranging from the declaration that Christ was mistaken to believe in demon possession[5]
to asserting that his resurrection was a pipe dream of the disciples. But whatever Bishop Spong said, I could generally bet
that no interviewer would raise the question of *why* he is both-
ering to be a bishop at all.

It's a good question. After all, if Jesus is not the one true
incarnate God of Israel and his bodily resurrection never happened, why does Bishop Spong retain a position whose central
purpose is to teach what he adamantly insists is untrue? It seems
rather like remaining the chairman of the Flat Earth Society,
sworn to uphold the teaching and doctrines of Flat Earthism,
while simultaneously pouring forth book after book utterly repudiating it. Yet, despite all this contradiction, all is tranquil.
Nobody asks why he is still a bishop and he does not remind us
to ask (perhaps because people are much less inclined to buy
books called *A Plumber Rethinks the Birth of Jesus* or *A Park-
ing Lot Attendant Rethinks the Meaning of Scripture*).

This ingenious (and lucrative) artistry has not gone unno-
ticed by others in the world of modernist showmanship who
style themselves as the Jesus Seminar. Presenting themselves as
pure practitioners of the best and brightest in current biblical

research, this conclave of academics (headed by Robert Funk and John Dominic Crossan) claims that "the scholarship represented by the Fellows of the Jesus Seminar is the kind that has come to prevail in all the great universities of the world."[6] And on the strength of this claim they have had an exciting time in the media since the mid-1980s, claiming to know just what Jesus did (or more precisely, did *not*) say and do. Thus, via carefully managed press releases, the public has been steadily informed with "eye-catching progress reports on the work of the Jesus Seminar under headlines such as 'Most of Jesus' words ghostwritten,' 'Jesus probably didn't recite Lord's Prayer, scholars say,' 'Is the Bible the gospel truth?', and 'Scholars compiling new Bible' "[7] all leading up to the much-ballyhooed release of their book *The Five Gospels: The Search for the Authentic Words of Jesus.*

Before we look at this "search" further, it is important to point out that mainstream biblical scholars find the Jesus Seminar's claims of rigorous, broad-based scholarship to be laughable. Richard B. Hays, Associate Professor of New Testament at the Divinity School of Duke University, points out that:

> Not one member of the New Testament faculty from Yale, Harvard, Princeton, Duke, University of Chicago, Union Theological Seminary, Vanderbilt, SMU, or Catholic University is involved in this project. It goes without saying that faculties of evangelical seminaries are not represented here. Nor are any major scholars from England or the Continent.[8]

Thus, it is not terribly surprising to discover that the great university scholars the Jesus Seminar claims to represent have a markedly different attitude toward these self-appointed spokespersons for True Biblical Scholarship.

> In fact — let it be said clearly — most professional biblical scholars are profoundly skeptical of the methods and conclusions of this academic splinter group . . . . The point is simply that this imaginative book has been produced by a self-selected body of scholars who hold a set of unconventional views about Jesus and the gospels. They are of course free to publish these views; however, their attempt to present these views as "the assured results of critical scholarship" is — one must say it — reprehensible deception.[9]

And well such professional biblical scholars might be skeptical. For the fact is, the Jesus Seminar's method for discerning which of the words of Jesus are "truly authentic" is curious indeed. In a nutshell, the Seminar declares that any saying reported of Christ by the gospels which reflects teaching also found in the New Testament Church *must* be a fiction placed on the lips of Christ by early Christians:

> Sayings and parables expressed in "Christian" language are the creation of the evangelists or their Christian predecessor. . . . This axiom bears repeating: Jesus was not the first Christian . . . . *The contrast between Christian language or viewpoint and the language or viewpoint of Jesus is a very important clue to the real voice of Jesus.*[10] [italics added]

Thus, the Jesus Seminar claims to know Jesus did not, for instance, say "Take, eat: this is my body" at the Last Supper precisely *because* the entire early Church reports that he did. Similarly, he had no interest in the Day of the Lord precisely *because* every other Jew did. For by an equally strange method of reasoning, the Jesus Seminar also decrees that anything Jesus is reported as saying which has roots in Judaism is unauthentic too (apparently on the grounds that Jesus couldn't possibly have agreed with his fellow Jews about anything at all). In short, a gospel saying of Jesus is authentic only when it is bears no resemblance whatever either to the culture in which he lived or to the teaching of the New Testament Church which is profoundly devoted to his memory.

So then, once we have neatly snipped away every source that an ordinary historian would look to for evidence about his subject, who, according to the Jesus Seminar, is this "authentic Jesus"? Oddly enough, he looks very much like someone the Jesus Seminar would approve of. We are told that:

> "He was a traveling sage who traded in wisdom." The description pegs him — as some of the Seminar members have argued in other publications — as an itinerant Cynic philosopher, rather than as a prophet or the leader of a religious reform movement . . . . He never spoke about himself, however, or claimed to play any distinctive role in the consummation of God's purposes. Certainly he never claimed to be the Messiah.[11]

Thus, in the modernist wonderland of *The Five Gospels*, the "enigmatic sage from Nazareth" is a man as disconnected from his Jewish roots as he is from the Church which mistook him for God. He is portrayed as a "Cynic philosopher with no concern about Israel's destiny, no connection with the concerns and hopes that animated his Jewish contemporaries, no interest in the interpretation of Scripture, and no message of God's coming eschatological judgment."[12] The picture is of a sort of befuddled mystic, able to peer into the heart of the cosmic drama and to perceive the mind of God in a way not given to most mortals:

> God was so real for him that he could not distinguish God's present activity from any future activity. He had a poetic sense of time in which the future and the present merged, simply melted together, in the intensity of his vision.[13]

Sadly, however, Jesus had neither a Ph.D. like the authors of *The Five Gospels* nor the good fortune to have the members of the Jesus Seminar in his circle of friends. Instead he had only Galilean peasants whom he had handpicked, all without Ph.D.s as well. And because of all this, Jesus, the brilliant and profoundly wise sage, was somehow strangely hindered from noticing that his apostles were not merely unclever, but were without question the twelve stupidest men on the planet — men who would quickly forget virtually everything he said and did. Which is, of course, why we need the services of the Jesus Seminar. For, to put it bluntly, we ordinary believers who gape and grin and believe Christ came down from heaven are also ignorant and not terribly bright:

> After all, as we are informed in *The Five Gospels*, "the Christ of creed and dogma, who had been firmly in place in the Middle Ages, can no longer command the assent of those who have seen the heavens through Galileo's telescope."[14]

In other words, the members of the Jesus Seminar know that the Earth goes around the sun (as we ordinary believers do not) and, by a wonderful alchemy of reason, they have deduced from this piece of arcane physics the remarkable conclusion that Jesus is therefore not God. What is more, they have done so because, unlike you and me, they and their Scholars' Version of the Bible are:

> free of ecclesiastical and religious control, unlike other major translations into English, including the King James Version and its descendants (Protestant), the Douay-Rheims Version and its progeny (Catholic), and the New International Version (Evangelical) . . . The Scholars' Version is authorized by scholars.[15]

In short, the members of the Jesus Seminar, like Dr. Science, Know More Than You Do. In fact, they even know more than the people who actually knew Jesus and shared his culture, language, table, and trials. The Jesus Seminar knows that the apostles, not having Ph.D.s or telescopes, were cruelly hampered in their ability to recall even a little of the most compelling figure they ever knew, just as you and I and all others without Ph.D.s and telescopes are wholly unable to recall anything at all about our favorite teacher, our first love, or our own mothers and fathers.

Thus, the Jesus Seminar, like most modernists, asks us to believe that the Misunderstood Sage of Nazareth was a figure so riveting, inspiring, charismatic, and mesmerizing that he galvanized a movement of deeply devoted disciples into ignoring everything he said and did, utterly forgetting his unforgettable oratory and replacing it with reams of quotations and stories about him having the historical value of a fever dream. It proposes that, though he never walked on water or calmed a storm, the Jesus of modernism is nonetheless a miracle worker of sorts. Simply by uttering a few sketchy epigrams about being nice, this itinerant preacher (who did *not*, we are assured, make claims of deity, multiply loaves, raise the dead, or even compose the "Lord's Prayer") managed to transform pious Jewish monotheists into men who willingly blasphemed the God he preached by deifying this Nazarene cipher. So deeply inspired by the awesome figure of Jesus were they that, out of profound reverence for Him, they obliterated virtually every trace of his memory and substituted in its place the ingenious fabrication called the gospel.

So (according to modernism) there is a radical discontinuity between the Jesus of history and the "Christ of faith." But (lest this disturb the ordinary faithful who still fancy the sun goes around the earth) we must here enter into what these scholars delicately refer to as the "Easter Event."

What might that be? Well, it's far too subtle for someone as ignorant as you and me to understand, but in modernist bafflegab it goes something like this: the Resurrection (and the entire gospel) is a mythic expression of the gestalt of messianic expectation alloyed with Yahwist apocalyptic, pagan fertility myth, and certain psychological factors catalyzed by the Christ event and finding its locus in the transsignification of the Christian community's own self-empowering transcendence of the death of Jesus of Nazareth and exaltation of his ministry into a mode of "divine revelation."

Translation: the real Jesus (whoever he was) is dead as a doornail and was probably eaten by wild dogs soon after the crucifixion, according to John Dominic Crossan. But since the apostles believed in him real hard and created the gospel story out of thin air to relieve their guilt, disappointment, and religious psychosis, then we can say the Resurrection is "true" and full of "hope" in some incoherent sense.

> What actually and historically happened to the body of Jesus can best be judged from watching how later Christian accounts slowly but steadily increased the reverential dignity of their burial accounts. But what was there at the beginning that necessitated such an intensive volume of apologetic insistence? If the Romans did

not observe the Deuteronomic decree, Jesus' body would have been left on the cross for the wild beasts. And his followers, who had fled, would know that. If the Romans did observe the decree, the soldiers would have made certain Jesus was dead and then buried him themselves as part of their job. In either case, his body left on the cross or in a shallow grave barely covered with dirt and stones, the dogs were waiting. And his followers, who had fled, would know that too. Watch, then, how the horror of that brutal truth is sublimated through hope and imagination into its opposite.[16]

Some people refer to this as "scholarship illuminating the darkness of religious ignorance." For my part, I find it simply baffling. I can understand the village atheist saying boldly, "Christianity is just so much rot" and trampling a Bible underfoot. I can also see taking the text seriously when Paul says the Resurrection really happened and he knows five hundred people who can back him up (1 Cor 15:3-6). But to say, "It's all rot unless you believe in your heart that it isn't" is just incomprehensible. It's like saying that wishing will make the moon into green cheese. "Hope and imagination" indeed! Such statements look indistinguishable from my Mom's words to my brother when he was confronted with the shattering news that Santa Claus was not real. "Mike," she said, "If you *believe* he's real, then he is."

My finely tuned kid radar could immediately spot my mother's reply as one of those content-free "comforting" things parents say in order to keep children from bugging them too much. And my finely tuned Evangelical grown-up radar couldn't help but spot a similar evasion when modernist scholars, consigning the corpse of Jesus to wild dogs and chalking the Resurrection up to delusion, lies, and religious psychosis, sugarcoat all this with pious prattle about warm and fuzzy Easter Events born of "hope and imagination." It looks very much as though they are treating us ordinary believers like children who threaten to bug them too much and jeopardize their job security.

Yet, my Evangelical blood insisted, bug them we must. For something about their extremely brilliant scholarship seems both unsound and motivated by less-than-untrammeled devotion to the highest ideals. For as Robert Funk, one of the cochairs of the Jesus Seminar writes:

> If we are to survive as scholars of the humanities, as well as theologians, we must quit the academic closet. And we must begin to sell a product that has some utilitarian value to someone — or which at least appears to have utilitarian value to someone.[17]

Which is perhaps why these scholars, in their burning love of truth, are reportedly negotiating with Hollywood to transform their "assured results of critical scholarship" into a Tinseltown screenplay.[18] It was also perhaps why, for some reason, I couldn't shake the odd feeling that modernism was breeding well-heeled versions of the apocryphal pompadoured televangelist huckster. In a fashion rather reminiscent of the mythical Brother Bubba's Infomercial Gospel Hour, modernism cheesily retains the form of the gospel while refusing to believe a syllable of it. Indeed, modernism's spokespersons look for all the world like Brother Bubbas in tweed and turtlenecks: ever more adept at using Christian language to acquire tenure, book, and screenplay royalties, honoraria, speaker's fees, and media acclaim — all while spitting in the eye of the Faith. The only real difference is that Brother Bubba is, by and large, a fictitious whipping boy for those who want to trash ordinary believers, while the Jesus Seminar actually exists in all its lucrative cynicism.

But far worse than bilking people out of their cash is bilking believers (especially new and wobbly believers) out of their faith. Of such false prophets Scripture warns: "They will secretly introduce destructive heresies, even denying the sovereign Lord who bought them — bringing swift destruction on themselves. Many will follow their shameful ways and will bring the way of truth into disrepute. In their greed these teachers will exploit you with stories they have made up" (2 Pt 2:1-3).

Scripture is right, of course. For with their claims that biblical revelation is wholly replaceable by their human traditions of a gnostic or secular Jesus, they make the way fatally easy for young believers and seekers, struggling against sin and trying to become rooted in faith, to throw in the towel, laugh bitterly at being snookered by this religion thing, and retire forever into the cold embrace of secular despair. As Scripture warns, the net effect of such human traditions is to appeal "to the lustful desires of sinful human nature [and] entice people who are just escaping" from error (2 Pt 2:18).

This brought my Evangelical whimsy to a screeching halt. It was one thing to chuckle at the folly of academics and clerics. But it was quite another to sit idly by while one after another of Christ's little ones perished (and one after another of these false modernist prophets he died for staged the ultimate media event of tying a millstone around their own necks and plunging themselves into the sea). Something had to be done, and Scripture was clear what that was. According to the word, believers are to always be prepared to give a reason for the hope that we have (1 Pt 3:15). Therefore it seemed to be incumbent upon me as a believer to find the Christian reply to this denigration of the Faith — if only so I might be of some use to my local church should the rains come and the storms blow and some young believer get thrown into a tizzy by watching some tweedy Professor Bubba on the *Today Show*.

So I sat down and started thinking through a reply to the arguments of the debunkers. In doing so, I assumed, like a good

Evangelical, that the battle lines were clear: the Bible *vs.* the traditions of men.

I was right. But only partly.

NOTES

1. "Man is destined to die once, and after that to face judgment" (Heb 9:27).
2. John Shelby Spong, *Rescuing the Bible from Fundamentalism: A Bishop Rethinks the Meaning of Scripture* (New York: HarperCollins, 1991), pp. 116-118.
3. John Shelby Spong. *Born of a Woman: A Bishop Rethinks the Birth of Jesus* (New York: HarperCollins, 1992), p. 3.
4. Spong, *Born of a Woman: A Bishop Rethinks the Birth of Jesus*, pp. 126-128.
5. "He obviously didn't know about epilepsy because He was wrong about it." in "The Door Interview: Dr. John Shelby Spong," *The Door*, #127 (January/February 1993), p. 8.
6. Richard B. Hays, "The Corrected Jesus," *First Things*, No. 43 (May 1994), p. 47.
7. Hays, "The Corrected Jesus," p. 43.
8. Hays, "The Corrected Jesus," p. 47.
9. Hays, "The Corrected Jesus," p. 47.
10. Robert W. Funk, Roy W. Hoover, and the Jesus Seminar. *The Five Gospels: The Search for the Authentic Words of Jesus* (New York: Macmillan, 1993), pp. 24-25 (italics mine).
11. Hays, "The Corrected Jesus," p. 47.
12. Hays, "The Corrected Jesus," p. 47.
13. Hays, "The Corrected Jesus," p. 45.
14. Hays, "The Corrected Jesus," p. 48.
15. Funk, Hoover, and the Jesus Seminar. *The Five Gospels: The Search for the Authentic Words of Jesus*, p. xviii.
16. John Dominic Crossan, *Jesus: A Revolutionary Biography* (New York: HarperCollins Publishers, 1994), p. 154.
17. Hays, "The Corrected Jesus," p. 48.
18. Hays, "The Corrected Jesus," p. 48.

Chapter Two
A Commonsense Look
at
Jesus of Nazareth

Aut Deus aut homo malus — "Either God or a bad man."

W hen I began to ponder an argument against the human traditions of the modernists, I found it was their uniform *hastiness* that most irritated me. It is perhaps a curious thing to speak of a hasty tradition, but it is entirely accurate here. Much of the modernists' method seemed to consist of cobbling together simplistic denials of the plain meaning of Scripture, all turning on the twentieth century habit of having a facile explanation for everything supernatural, provided it explains the supernatural away. And this method is thoroughly traditional in that it endlessly repeats these little denials in a sort of litany until people are imbued with the fixed sense that something real has been said, some foundation has been laid and some mighty edifice of Current Biblical Research has been erected.

This came home to me one day as I listened to a member of the Jesus Seminar on a secular talk radio show. A caller asked him if there was any "proof" that Jesus had multiplied loaves and fishes. (I don't know if he expected the Jesus Seminar man to suddenly produce a two-thousand-year-old dried trout and slap it against the microphone or what.) But at any rate, the Jesus Seminar man, instead of saying, "All we have in evidence of this is the teaching of the New Testament documents," said in essence, "We now know the nature miracles of Christ (walking on water, multiplying loaves and fishes, etc.) are not to be taken as literal events. They are instead parables told in dramatic form by the evangelist to make a spiritual point about Jesus."

Now before we are lulled into a hypnotic stupor by the singsong of these words, let us pinch ourselves or plunge our heads into cold water for a moment and ask two simple questions:

How does he *know*? How *could* he know that the nature miracles recorded by the gospels are merely "enacted parables" invented by the evangelist to make a point about Jesus?

After all, the only thing this man has to go on is the biblical text. Yet the biblical text says nothing to support his theoretical assertion. There are no asterisked parchments in Luke's hand recording his soothing clarification, "This miracle account is intended to be allegorical." There are no yellow sticky notes from Peter attached to the *Codex Vaticanus* saying, "Mark is speaking metaphorically here." In short, there is not one grain of hard evidence that the miracle stories are fictitious. There is only a modernist prejudice against miracles.

Yet the talk show scholar did not even inform the caller that he was offering theory. He simply bowled the man over with his impressive credentials, like a peacock establishing dominance over a rival male, and asserted this utterly unsubstantiated theory as "the latest scholarship." And after this display of academic plumage, the already uninformed caller announced his even more profoundly uninformed new conviction, "So then, modern scholarship really *has* disproved the official story of the Church!" He then thanked the talk-show scholar and went away rejoicing, believing nothing.

As I listened, my first instinct was to say, "Hey! Wait a

minute. Before we get swept up in this frenzy of theological slam dancing and gleefully destroy the 'official story,' we ought to find out what it is we are destroying. Then, if we still want to smash the Pieta or spray-paint the Last Supper, we shall at least know what we are destroying. Better still, if we familiarize ourselves with the Christian story again, we may in fact find that the Bible explains itself in a way that the human tradition of modernism doesn't. In fact, I think we'll find that the Bible explains itself without the need of any tradition at all!"

But to do that, it seemed to me, we need to begin, not with an official anything, nor with the concealed prejudices of pedants, but with a question from Scripture itself, a question put to me by my own Evangelical tutors in the faith long ago. A question which, as they taught me well, becomes an intractable question until we have either answered it to our heart's ease and our soul's salvation or else shut it out with distraction and will power.

The question is this: *"Who do you say I am?"*

The questioner is Jesus of Nazareth and the people who report the question (and other rather odd things about the questioner) are the gospel writers.

Now as an unbeliever, I had been confronted with the gospel and with this question for the first time. And I could see only two options:

1. Believe Jesus is the Son of God (and therefore pay rather careful attention to him and whoever he speaks well of); or,
2. Don't.

The second option seems a lot simpler to many people, but it doesn't really answer Jesus' question, which is a toughie. For, if we deny that Jesus is the Son of God, then we have to say what he really was. Yet, judging from the record preserved in the New Testament, all the alternatives appear lame to me. For if those records are accurate (as we shall, for the moment, assume), we have only a few options to consider.

Mr. Nice Guy?

Maybe Jesus was not really divine, but rather was a great teacher and moral exemplar, a real swell guy who was nonetheless, merely human.

The difficulty with this theory is the little matter of his claim to deity. Real swell guys are generally able to distinguish between their puny human selves and the God of the Universe. Indeed, the more swell they are, the more acutely aware they are of the fact that they are only human. Yet Jesus of Nazareth claims for himself the name "I AM" which is the very name of God in the Hebrew language (Jn 8:58). He announces that he is "Lord of the Sabbath." (Mk 2:28). He forgives sins (including the sins of total strangers who have never harmed him personally); which is to say, he claims to be the Judge of the human race (Mk 2:1-12). He makes this even more explicit by claiming the messianic title of "Son of Man" and declaring (in the parable of the sheep and the goats) that he will come at the end of time to judge the world (Mt 25:31-46). He declares that he is "the Son" who alone knows the Father and who alone can make the Father known (Lk 10:22). And when he is confronted point blank concerning these claims in a trial at which his life hangs in the balance, he bluntly reasserts them (Mk 14:61-62). So the Mr. Nice Guy hypothesis is a bit weak.

New Age Guru?

Some modern folks (largely confined to about the last two decades and largely located in the audiences of New Age speakers) have attempted to put a slightly different spin on the Nice Guy hypothesis by saying that Jesus' claim to deity was intended "in an Eastern sense." By this it is generally meant that Jesus had somehow fallen under the influence of some variant of pantheistic belief and was, in fact, merely asserting his "God consciousness" in an attempt to awaken this same consciousness in his benighted peers. He was, in short, attempting to be a guru to the Jews. Jesus, says the average New Age spokesperson, did not mean that he and he alone is the God of Israel and the Transcendent Creator of Heaven and Earth as we crude westerners misunderstood him to say. On the contrary, when he says he is the Son of God, he means we are *all* children of God and indeed, we are God ourselves if we but realize it. It's just that the primitive Jewish mind was unable to comprehend this higher truth.

The problems with this theory are numerous. For there is simply not a single gossamer thread of evidence that the thoroughly Jewish, Scripture-soaked Jesus of Nazareth was even *slightly* influenced by pantheist philosophy, much less bent on completely revolutionizing Judaism into a religion that identifies God with the world. On the contrary, he affirms that God is *Lord* of heaven and earth, not that he *is* heaven and earth as pantheism asserts (Lk 10:21). Indeed, in the length and breadth of his preaching, we do not find the slightest hint that he conceives of either God or human beings in Eastern categories. He does not speak of God as identical with Creation; he speaks of him in a thoroughly Jewish sense as Transcendent Creator, Judge, and Father (Mt 19:4; 6:14-15). He does not conceive of his disciples as parts of God who have only to realize their own Godhead by letting go of their false consciousness of guilt and sin. Rather, he plainly reminds them they are sinners in need of salvation who are, apart from him alone, incapable of accomplishing that salvation or anything else (Jn 15:5). So far from affirming that We're Okay and He's Okay, he frequently reminds us that we are sinners, but he is without sin; we are from below, but he is from above (Jn 8:1-11; 8:23). He insists that the way to life is not via self-affirmation of our own intrinsic divinity but self-denial for his sake, who alone is one with the Father (Mt 16:24-26; Jn 10:30). None of this squares very easily with the notion that Christ was really just trying to awaken us to our own deity. Quite the contrary, it looks as though he was attempting to alert us exclusively to his.

Lying Publicity Hound?

But, says the modern mind, telling me I'm Not Okay isn't polite! And telling me I am from below while he is from above is elitist! Thus, some offended modern souls offer yet another theory: maybe he wasn't so nice, after all. Maybe, in fact, he was downright tacky: a man who began as a pushy and insulting blusterer, and who came close to starting a local cult of worship round himself in the hopes of gaining gold, guns, and girls. Maybe he was just a clever huckster bent on selling himself to the yokels and the ruling classes, both Roman and Jewish, for the usual reasons of political clout and a shot at getting rich or famous quick.

The problem with this theory is that, for the past century, those who disliked him most did so for diametrically opposite reasons than this theory proposes. They despised him, not for his strutting egoism, but for his humility and seemingly overpatient counsels which, as G.K. Chesterton observed, might be taken as an attempt to make a man too like a sheep. Thus, proponents of the Lying Publicity Hound theory must take it up, not with Christianity, but with Christianity's bitterest enemies of the nineteenth and twentieth centuries, such as Marx and Nietzsche. These men and their devotees loathed Christ's *meekness* and focused relentlessly on his (and Christendom's) "failure" to demand revolt among the oppressed masses and his "weak and slavish" counsels to turn the other cheek; counsels he clearly kept himself.

That is why in the New Testament record we find him so politically unassertive that he tends to flee into the desert when people try to make him king (Jn 6:15). Then when they catch up with him, he turns and makes speeches (such as his Bread of Life discourse [Jn 6:25-60]) which are guaranteed to repulse and offend all but the most diehard grass-roots supporters. He also repeatedly does everything he can to conceal his miracles (Mk 5:43; 7:36; Lk 5:14), hardly the actions of a publicity hound. Odder still (for someone with an egomaniacal lust for power), he has a penchant for coupling his most extreme claims with a peculiar naïveté (or was it goodness?) that exalts the outcast and casts out the exalted (which, as every egomaniac knows, is not the way to get ahead in life).

For instance, he hobnobs with slobs, pimps, and drunks. He surrounds himself with tacky people who look terrible in campaign brochures and treats them, not as helpless beneficiaries of his largesse (which a self-aggrandizer *would* do), but as disciples whom he takes seriously and trusts (Jn 15:15). He looks past the President of the Capernaum Chamber of Commerce (the sort of man who has an Important Theory About How to Deal With the Lower Social Orders), smiles broadly and, without excusing himself, extends a warm, cheery "Hello!" to the local hooker who just crashed the exclusive cocktail party without an invitation (Lk 7:36-50). Whatever else this is, it is not the behavior of any self-aggrandizer I've ever seen. Simply put, those who regard themselves as Great Men take great care to cement the same impression in everyone else's mind, and particularly in the minds of those who are most powerful. They shun the opportunity to be associated in the public mind with the likes of Simon the Zealot, Mary Magdalene, or those hick fishermen from Galilee who speak with a twang.

Jesus, however, did not seem to give a rip what people thought of him. And he seemed particularly at pains to make sure that those Romans and Jews who thought the least of him, and had the power to do something about it, would find plenty of reasons (and opportunities) to see him dead.

None of this squares easily with the self-aggrandizer theory. What it does square with is the blunt claim by Christ that the Son of Man came to seek and save that which was lost, to give his life as a ransom for many (Mk 10:45).

Indeed, even his outbursts of anger seem to have been remarkably unconscious of political strategizing and much more in line with the orthodox Christian picture of Jesus as a man totally in love with God and deeply enraged by the betrayal of that love by the religious jet set of his day. His first act upon entering Jerusalem in triumph was to attack, not the Romans (as an ambitious political leader would have), but the moneychangers and the Temple elite (Lk 19:45), thus applying the coup de grace to any possibility of befriending the people most likely to be of help in raising a popular rebellion against Rome (as Bar-Kochba was to attempt a century later).

This political "blunder" is typical of what marked his entire career. He was forever alienating the most powerful men of his day, both Jewish and, when he came to trial, Roman.

> Again the high priest asked him, "Are you the Christ, the Son of the Blessed One?"
> "I am," said Jesus (Mk 14:61-62).

> "Are you the king of the Jews?" asked Pilate.
> "Yes, it is as you say," Jesus replied (Mk 15:2).

He thereby invited crucifixion after having annihilated any support from his own countrymen. Altogether *not* the actions of a self-aggrandizer.

Indeed, upon close inspection, *nothing* in his actions indicates he sought power and domination at all. Rather, he seemed to speak as though he already *had* all power and was here to give it (and his life) away to whoever would listen to him, even if they were factory rejects, tax collectors, and general losers. In a very peculiar sense, he seems to have *wanted* nothing, nothing earthly, at any rate.

> "My kingdom is not of this world. If it were, my servants would fight to prevent my arrest by the Jews. But now my kingdom is from another place" (Jn 18:36).

There is a strange self-possession in his most extreme claims which demands a response from us but does not, in any way, *depend* on one. Rather, he repeatedly scandalizes even his most devoted disciples and watches coolly as they react in shock and confusion to his declarations about himself. He makes no apologies as his disciples leave in droves (Jn 6:60-64), his enemies sour on him (Lk 11:37-53), and his family tactfully suggests he might be a candidate for the madhouse (Mk 3:21). Nothing deters him from his set course, yet his course is set, not for a seat at the palace or a gig as a featured guest on the talk show circuit, but for a horsewhipping and a shameful death, mother-naked and covered only with a crown of thorns, his own blood, and the spit of his bitterest enemies.

This is not the sort of glory Great Men envision for themselves when they give after-dinner talks about their Sense of Destiny, the Rightness of Their Cause and the Bright Future they promise. But it is emphatically the thing that Jesus repeatedly prophesied and deliberately chose to embrace (though he feared it). Again and again he plainly taught that he would be rejected by the scribes and Pharisees and put to death (Mk 8:31; 9:12; 9:31-32). Repeatedly, he made references, both direct and oblique, to his rendezvous with death. He spoke to his future murderers of "destroying the Temple" of his body, words which were misunderstood and used against him at his trial (Jn 2:19-21; Mk 14:58). He spoke of being "lifted up" on the cross (Jn 3:14; 12:32-33). He praised Mary of Bethany for anointing his body for burial beforehand (Jn 12:7). He astonished his disciples by deliberately going to Jerusalem when his enemies were arrayed against him there (Mk 10:32-34). He spoke of his body broken and his blood shed the evening before his crucifixion (Mk 14:22-24). And he did it all, not out of a sense of megalomaniacal invulnerability but precisely because, as he said, "no prophet can die outside Jerusalem" (Lk 13:33).

In short, unlike Great Men, Jesus consistently acted as though revilement and death in obscurity were what he was born for. And he let nothing, including the pleas of those closest to him, hinder him in his strange mission (Mk 8:31-33). In some mysterious way, he regarded himself as profoundly *involved* in the human race, as though his obscure death on a hillside at the outskirts of the civilized world was somehow the key to unlocking the mystery of every human life. He spoke of his life as a "ransom" (Mk 10:45). He taught his disciples, on the very eve of his death, that his blood was "the blood of the covenant, which is poured out for many for the forgiveness of sins" (Mt 26:28). Everything we know of him points to this humiliation as the only sort of glory he ever sought. Which leaves one option open for the determined unbeliever. . . .

Insane?

Perhaps Jesus is just a candidate for the goofy booth; a frenzied monomaniac locked into one single solitary staring obsession with himself that crushed all sanity under the smothering hallucination that he was the absolute center of the Universe, the God of all Creation. After all, madmen frequently do strange things out of an excessive self-absorption which cares nothing about the reactions of others. Might he not be one of these mad zealots, driven round the bend by too much time in the desert and too much Messianic fervor?

Well, consider the Sermon on the Mount in Matthew 5-7. Does it look to you like the ravings of a lunatic? Read the sharp analysis and denunciation of the foibles of the powerful in Matthew 23 (an analysis as sharp as anything H.L. Mencken ever penned). Clear from your mind the fact that the stories are old and read again the account of his deft reply to the spin doctors who wanted to trip him up over paying taxes to Caesar (Mk 12:13-17). Observe again the brilliance and subtlety of his answer to those who wanted to stone the woman taken in adultery (Jn 8:1-11). These are, among other things, typical examples of a sharpness and think-on-your-feet sanity almost unheard of among mortals, yet which seemed to typify his uniquely Jewish savvy. In short, there seemed to be a *reason* why the people who tried to trick him were "astonished by his answer [and] became silent" (Lk 20:26). There is a lucidity and fresh-air sense of perspective, irony, and humor in him which is singularly lacking in the self-obsession of a religious fanatic like David Koresh. Would that we all were as mad as the Nazarene!

Consider also the curious ambiguity of his rendezvous with death. On the one hand, he sets his course for it with an iron resolve. But we never get the impression that he *desires* death or dallies with it the way a morbid romantic would. He does not rhapsodize about the joys of death. He is not a pessimist or philosopher who seeks death as an escape. Rather, as C.S. Lewis observes, Jesus "detested this penal obscenity not less than we do, but more."[1] He weeps at the grave of Lazarus (Jn 11:35). When it comes to the point of his own death, he sweats blood and begs God to be spared (Lk 22:41-44). But when the divine refusal comes he goes through with the thing. Why?

Well, not because he has an insane death wish or suffocating obsession with himself. Rather, he looks more and more like a man *under orders*. A man who believes himself commanded by God to destroy the King of Death himself in mortal combat. In some ways he looks a great deal like the hero of a fairy tale. But he is not Jack the Giant Killer, living "once upon a time." He is a real human being who really lived.

Very well then, if the records are reliable they clearly show us a man who is neither merely nice, nor a liar, nor mad. Yet he still stands there before us implacably asking, "Who do you say I am?" (Mt 16:15). And as he does so in an ever more insistent voice, we begin to feel the grip of C.S. Lewis' logic that:

> The historical difficulty of giving for the life, sayings and influence of Jesus any explanation that is not harder than the Christian explanation is very great. The discrepancy between the depth and sanity and (let me add) *shrewdness* of his moral teaching and the rampant megalomania which must lie behind his theological teaching unless

he is indeed God, has never been satisfac-
torily got over.[2]

Thus far the evidence of the New Testament witnesses. But, of course, the question then becomes "Why should we trust these witnesses? Why believe the testimony of a community of Jesus worshipers who are, it is asserted by the skeptic, fudging the facts and embellishing the tale to suit their rapidly expanding cult surrounding this divinized rabbi? Is this not trusting in a rather prejudiced witness?"

This is a good question. So let us ask it.

NOTES

1. C.S. Lewis, *Miracles* (New York: Macmillan, 1947), p. 125.
2. Lewis, *Miracles*, pp. 108-109.

CHAPTER THREE
FAMOUS LAST WORDS

They couldn't hit an elephant at this dist —
— The last words of Union General John B. Sedgwick,
rallying the troops at the Battle of Spotsylvania, 1864

Why should we trust the veracity of disciples who report Jesus of Nazareth's words and deeds? To begin with, let us remember also that to ask this is to ask (just as we asked of Jesus), "What sort of people *were* these early Christians, both apostles and the circle that surrounded them? Were they enthusiasts who just got a bit excited and mistook their rabbi for God?"

Actually if there is any impression of the disciples that most clearly stands out from the gospel accounts, it is of a group of rather obtuse people who, so far from reckless enthusiasm, are about as pedestrian as can be. Again and again, Jesus can be seen with his eyes rolling, sighing "Do you *still* not understand?" (Mk 8:21). This affords occasional comic relief in the gospels, as when (after feeding five thousand people with a few loaves of bread) Jesus warns the disciples to "beware of the leaven of the Pharisees and the leaven of Herod" (Mk 8:15 RSV). His disciples' insightful response? "They discussed this with one another and said, 'It is because we have no bread' " (Mk 8:16).

Clearly we are not dealing with theological rocket scientists here. Nor do they come off as men inclined to read undue significance into things, much less read into his life an all-embracing transcendence that consummated all Scripture, all Jewish heritage, explained the deepest things of the universe, and fired them with certainty that this man was the Lord of all and the Conqueror of Death. This is abundantly clear from the biblical documents which continually paint a picture of the apostles as guys who were slow on the uptake, as lummoxes who repeatedly squabbled over who was the greatest (Mk 9:33-34), and as cowards who abandoned the one they loved at the moment of his supreme crisis (Mk 14:50).

It is this stark portrayal of the disciples which also makes it difficult to believe the next alternative explanation: namely that Jesus was a sort of religious President Ulysses S. Grant — a pious rabbi who meant well but who, with singular bad luck, managed to completely surround himself with the world's most brilliant liars and cynically opportunistic cult founders. These liars (so the theory goes) then faked the Resurrection, founded the Church, set themselves up as his oracles and God's Right Hand Men, and created the whole evil fiction of the gospel. They obliterated the memory of the historical Jesus and invented the alien dogmas of a deified Christ in order to control their snookered and illiterate converts.

Now our century has seen any number of liars and cult founders. Do the apostles resemble them? The movements founded by Stalin, Hitler, Mao, Pol Pot, Jim Jones, and the other tyrants and con artists of this bloodiest of centuries do not portray their founders as fools and all-too-fallible sinners. Yet the churches of the apostles carefully and even dogmatically incorporated into their official literature a stark record of their apostolic founders' oafish failures — *apparently at the insistence of the apostles themselves.*

To get the hang of how remarkable this is, imagine Communist Party meetings in the Soviet Union of the 1930s opening with regular readings of the cowardly deeds and stupidity of Joseph Stalin. Picture the Communist faithful urged to meditate on the ways in which Stalin and his fellow Communists misunderstood, resisted, denied, and betrayed the most elementary precepts of Marx the Father and of His only Son, Lenin. Yet it appears that something very much like this recounting of the spectacular failings of the apostles was established and repeated endlessly *by their very own preaching*. On the apostles' own authority, a careful reiteration of their tremendous and glaring faults was endlessly kneaded into the life of the whole Church from Day One, dutifully recorded in the gospels, and canonized as the very word of God by the people they converted.

This forces us to scrutinize the Apostolic Cultist theory with some skepticism. If the apostles are such cheesy hucksters why don't they act more like it? If they were ambitious con men, the gospels should read something like propaganda from the Stalin era: a tightly controlled portrayal of the apostles as Christ's Best Buddies and Tireless Servants. Instead we get embarrassing little vignettes like these:

- Jesus calling Peter the Chief Apostle "Satan." (Imagine Soviet literature in the '30s endlessly repeating a quotation in which Lenin rebukes Stalin as a "capitalist swine.") (Mk 8:33);
- Peter's squalid triple betrayal of Christ (one of them prompted by the Big Strong Fisherman's terror at the accusation of a servant girl [Mk 14:66-72]);
- Thomas and his doubts (Jn 11:16; 20:24-25);
- James and John and their grab for power and glory (and the fits of jealousy this gave the other apostles [Mk 10:35-41]);
- James and John urging Jesus to call down fire on the Samaritans (Lk 9:54);
- The Twelve's squabbles on the very eve of their Master's death (Lk 22:24) and their all-too-human failure to believe or even understand the Lord they are preaching (to say nothing of their cowardly abandonment of Jesus in his hour of most desperate peril [Mk 14:50]);
- The Twelve's failure to believe the witness of the women at the tomb, amounting to their total failure to believe the

promise of Resurrection which the disciples had heard from Christ's own lips (Lk 24:10-11). (By the way, a twentieth century audience, imbued from birth with a deep faith in the equality of the sexes, often fails to see the significance of the women's witness to the Resurrection. A first century patriarchal audience would scarcely fail to find incredible the testimony of peasant women, at least one, Mary Magdalene, with a shady psychological profile ["out of whom he had driven seven demons" (Mk 16:9)]. Why would cunning liars, fabricating a Resurrection, invent female witnesses at all . . . unless the story actually happened that way?);

- Paul's eager participation in the murder of Stephen and persecution of the Church (Acts 7:54-60; 8:1);
- Paul's rebuke of Peter's chickenhearted capitulation to the Judaizers (Gal 2:11-16);
- Paul's fight with Barnabas over the trustworthiness of Mark (Acts 15:36-39).

Cunning liars would also not be terribly likely to carefully preserve Mark's and Matthew's haunting record of Christ's last words: "My God, my God, why have you forsaken me?" (Mt 27:46; Mk 15:34). Surely, men who are out to snooker superstitious slaves don't put a cry of *despair* on the lips of their fictitious God figure. Nor would they continually put so many words of ignorance, stupidity, and betrayal on their own lips. No cult founders in any age allow themselves to be seen as human as these people do.

Yet the apostles (and, significantly, their devoted chroniclers such as Luke and Mark) never lose sight of their humanness. Indeed, they display it unaffectedly on every page of the gospels. Thus, the biblical witnesses, for all their astounding claims concerning the person of Christ, read like the words of people who act for all the world like honest, ordinary witnesses to honestly extraordinary events. Likewise, the first disciples they made (who will shortly join the apostles in persecution and death by the sword), make no effort to air brush the warts off the apostolic noses in the family album called the New Testament. Neither Luke nor Mark ever idealize the apostles as they are supposed to have idealized Christ. Indeed, they look less and less like they were even inclined to idealize *him*. For the gospels, so far from fiddling with the story to trim off the rough edges and deify their subject, seem to be adamant about preserving the fullness of the story even if it is difficult and embarrassing. Thus, they were astoundingly faithful in preserving, not only the scriptural witness to the failings of the apostles, but even those bits which seemed to threaten their claims of Christ's deity.

Take, for instance, the little nettlesome quotes such as " 'Why do you call me good?' Jesus answered, 'No one is good — except God alone' " (Mk 10:18); "He could not do any miracles there, except lay his hands on a few sick people and heal them" (Mk 6:5); "No one knows about that day or hour, not even the angels in heaven, nor the Son, but only the Father" (Mt 24:36); and "Who touched me?" (Lk 8:45). Such quotes appear to bear witness to Jesus' imperfection, weakness, and ignorance — not the sort of thing one wants in an idealized god figure.

Therefore the question remains. If these people were not religious maniacs, cultists, liars, fact-fudgers, or general fruitcakes, what were they? How did they create from thin air (as is asserted) the fable of the God-Man Christ and get people to believe in it and in them to the point of being willing martyrs for their faith? Ultimately we must face the same question from an apostle that we faced concerning their Master: "Who do you say I am?" And all the answers but one look ever more preposterous, till we are forced back to the ultimatum voiced by C.S. Lewis in *Mere Christianity*:

> A man who was merely a man and said the sort of things Jesus said would not be a great moral teacher. He would either be a lunatic — on a level with the man who says He is a poached egg — or else He would be the Devil of Hell. You must make your choice. Either

this man was, and is, the Son of God: or else a
madman or something worse. You can shut Him
up for a fool, you can spit at Him and kill Him
as a demon; or you can fall at His feet and call
Him Lord and God. But let us not come with
any patronizing nonsense about His being a
great teacher. He has not left that open to us.
He did not intend to.[1]

So I had the last word against the human tradition of modernism, no? I could now rally the Evangelical troops to battle, secure in the knowledge that my argument for the complete self-sufficiency of biblical revelation was bulletproof. Right?

Wrong. For modernism, so far from blinking, posed a very disturbing problem.

It's quite true, said a little modernist voice in my head, that Bishop Spong, the Jesus Seminar, and other modernists are, in fact, creating a human tradition rooted in human scholarship. Indeed, we don't quite see why you have spent so much energy pointing out what we have never denied. For as Robert Funk openly declares, "We need a new narrative of Jesus, a new gospel, if you will. . . ."[2] He does so because modernism frankly acknowledges that the gospel is nothing other than a human tradition. But don't kid us that *your* picture of Jesus stands in some sort of stark contrast to ours, because your view of Jesus is no less rooted in tradition than ours. For the fact is, the Bible upon which you just based your charming little apologetic contains the books it does, not because it fell from heaven, leather-bound and gold-embossed in 95 A.D., but because mere men decreed at the Councils of Hippo (in 393) and Carthage (in 397) that a lot of *other* early Christian writings were to be barred from the canon (writings like the Didache, the Gospel of Thomas, and the epistle of Barnabas to name just a few). But as truly free human beings, we are not constrained by such fallible human authorities as you still choose to venerate.

> Since the Scholar's Version is not bound by
> the dictates of church councils, its contents and
> organization vary from traditional bibles. . . .
> *The Five Gospels* contains the Gospel of Tho-
> mas in addition to the four canonical gospels.[3]

For we whom you call "modernists" prefer to be called "realists." We know that your view of Jesus depends entirely on
the claim of mere human beings that your canon of Scripture
and no other has the "true story" of Jesus. We know that many
of the books (such as the Gospel of Thomas) which were forbidden from the canon by mere men teach things not taught in
the traditional New Testament — things which give a very different impression of Jesus and his true followers indeed. We
know that your traditional canon of Scripture was compiled,
not by an angel, but by a slow, fumbling, and thoroughly human early Church hierarchy in a series of varying "canons"
which not only ruthlessly excluded alternative accounts such as
Thomas but also sometimes excluded books such as Hebrews,
James, 1 and 2 Peter, 3 John, Jude, and Revelation, and sometimes *included* books like the Apocalypse of Peter, the Shepherd of Hermas, and various deuterocanonical works. (Look it
up! It's in your own thoroughly Evangelical *New Bible Dictionary*!)[4]

Further, this traditional Church, in addition to formulating
the shape of your traditional Bible about *three hundred years*
after the death of the apostles, also declared a lot of other stuff
to be certain truths which even you regard as human tradition.
Or have you forgotten about purgatory, devotions to Mary
"sinless and ever-virgin Mother of God," prayers to the saints,
veneration of relics, icons and statues, the Sacrifice of the Mass,
adoration of the Eucharist as the True Body and Blood of Christ,
and such like? All these beliefs and practices were in full swing
and being taught by the very same Church that gave Scripture
its present shape. And that Scripture included, from the fourth
century to the Reformation, seven books (Tobit, Wisdom, Ju-

dith, 1 and 2 Maccabees, Sirach, and Baruch) and some pieces of Daniel and Esther which you Evangelicals reject as "apocryphal."

Therefore pardon me for saying so, said the voice of modernism, but it looks to us realists as though your own great Protestant theologian, R.C. Sproul, is more realistic than you. For he at least acknowledges the incoherence of your "purely biblical" revelation by describing your traditional Bible as a "fallible collection of infallible books"[5] (whatever that means).

"So then," asked the little voice of modernism in my head, *"Why precisely do you accept the present canon of biblical books as something other than human tradition?"*

Answer: I didn't have the faintest clue! Yet until that question could be answered clearly I realized that my "purely biblical" argument for Christianity was a series of neatly fashioned logic links attached to a hook hanging on a nail hammered firmly into . . . nothing. I had more thinking to do. A lot more.

NOTES

1. C.S. Lewis, *Mere Christianity, The Case for Christianity, Christian Behaviour,* and *Beyond Personality — Anniversary Edition* (New York: Macmillan, 1981), p. 45.
2. Richard B. Hays, "The Corrected Jesus," *First Things*, No. 43 (May 1994), p. 48.
3. Robert W. Funk, Roy W. Hoover, and the Jesus Seminar. *The Five Gospels: The Search for the Authentic Words of Jesus* (New York: Macmillan, 1993), p. xviii.
4. *New Bible Dictionary*, 2nd Edition, J.D. Douglas, Organizing Editor, (Wheaton: Tyndale House, 1984), pp. 171-176.
5. R.C. Sproul, "Scripture," *Roman Catholicism* (Orlando: Ligonier Ministries, 1988), audiotape series.

CHAPTER FOUR
BLIND ALLEYS

Houston, we've had a problem.
— *James Lovell, Apollo 13 Commander*

W hy is the canon of Scripture not a human tradition?" The question would not leave me alone.
It shook the foundations of what I had come to
believe when I had first become a Christian at the age of twenty.
Then and for many years after, I had rather absentmindedly
nodded assent to the general Evangelical sense that Scripture,
being "God-breathed," is therefore self-attesting and does not
depend at all upon tradition. For at the time of my conversion
my mind was primarily on Jesus, not on the question which now
irked and goaded me concerning canonicity. On the rare occasions when the issue of the canon *had* crossed my mind, I had
simply figured, "Since it's divinely inspired, it can be discerned
by any spirit-filled believer." I thought it was one of those "obvious" truths; the sort of thing you heard tossed around at Bible
studies and in sermons so often that you never gave it much
thought. Everyone knew what the Bible was, right?

The silence in my own heart was deafening.

So I began to puzzle this through, and in doing so, I thought
of Paul's dictum: "Test everything. Hold on to the good" (1
Thes 5:21). Presumably, I reasoned, "everything" includes the
supposed self-attestation of Scripture, so I sat down to think
and pray the thing through as honestly as I could. If the self-

attestation of Scripture held up, well and good. If not . . . well, I'd cross that bridge when I came to it.

So I began with the basic assertion I had heard times without number that the Scriptures bear witness to themselves. To this proposition I put the simple question, "Do they really?" and then sought in Scripture to see whether these things were so. In particular, I sought to know whether any inspired writer (or other biblical character) gave a clear teaching as to what, exactly, the canon of the holy Scriptures is.

I began with the question of the Old Testament. Jesus and the apostles, after all, commend "the Scriptures" to us and this means (for them) the Old Testament Scriptures. So I asked simply: does Scripture say what comprises the Old Testament? I set out searching for the solution to this riddle in a way which I thought would help me avoid any reliance on tradition. But it proved to be my first blind alley.

Blind Alley #1: No Inner Witness of the Spirit

Many of my Evangelical teachers, in response to this problem, suggested that inspired Scripture ought to "witness to my spirit" and that this was a valid way of discerning the Lord's voice in my daily walk. To back this up biblically, they quoted John's teaching concerning the guidance of the Spirit:

> I am writing these things to you about those
> who are trying to lead you astray. As for you,
> the anointing you received from him remains
> in you, and you do not need anyone to teach
> you (1 Jn 2:26-27).

On the strength of this, I was frequently taught that the one who had truly come to know Jesus could "just tell" the word of God when he or she saw it. You "just knew" the anointing was on it and your spirit, which shared that anointing, responded. Thus, you didn't need anybody, not even the Church, to tell you what was and wasn't the word of God. The Spirit of Christ in your heart told you; the "official canon" of the Church was a mere confirmation of this.

This was a good theory but it quickly slammed into two difficult facts: a devout little Albanian Christian named Mother Teresa and a devout big German Christian named Martin Luther. Even my Evangelical pastors acknowledged Mother Teresa as a mighty woman of God with a powerful anointing of the Spirit. But this diminutive spiritual giant calls such books as Sirach, Tobit, Wisdom, Judith, 1 and 2 Maccabees, and Baruch "inspired Scripture." So do a lot of other people I would hesitate to call pagans (like St. Augustine, St. Francis of Assisi, G.K. Chesterton, and Catherine de Hueck Doherty). Yet these books, which they call "deuterocanonical" and "inspired Scripture," we Evangelicals call "apocryphal" and reject from the canon of inspired Scripture. Why did we reject them? Well, because Luther and other Reformers did. However, as I discovered, this was not all Luther rejected from Scripture. For as we Evangelicals did with the apocrypha, so Luther did with the epistle of James.

To be sure, Luther *liked* the epistle of James, saying, "I praise it and consider it a good book,"[1] just as we Evangelicals thought the apocrypha good books. But that was about it. He certainly did not regard James as Scripture any more than we Evangelicals thought 1 Maccabees or *Mere Christianity* Scripture. As Luther himself said, "I do not regard [James] as the writing of an apostle" because he believed it "is flatly against St. Paul and all the rest of Scripture in ascribing justification to works."[2]

Thus, Luther's original *Preface to James' Epistle* argued that James:

> wanted to guard against those who relied on faith without works, but was unequal to the task. He tries to accomplish by harping on the law what the apostles accomplish by stimulating people to love. Therefore, I will not have him in my Bible to be numbered among the

> true chief books, though I would not thereby
> prevent anyone from including or extolling him,
> for there are otherwise many good things in
> him. "One man is no man" in worldly things;
> how, then, should this single man alone prevail
> against Paul and all the rest of Scripture?[3]

Likewise, in other writings he underscores this rejection of James from the New Testament, calling it "an epistle full of straw . . . for it has nothing of the nature of the gospel about it."[4]

So then, I had three riddles.

First, shouldn't the spirits of strong, committed Christians like Mother Teresa, Augustine, Francis of Assisi, and G.K. Chesterton recognize the non-inspiration of the apocrypha just as Luther's strongly committed Christian spirit did?

Second, if we were certain Luther's spirit had been right about the apocrypha, why were we equally certain his spirit was wrong about the epistle of James?

And third, how in the world was I supposed to arrive at an answer, especially since I was forced to admit that in my own reading I was not at all confident I felt my spirit whispering one peep about what was and wasn't canonical? Was one's heart supposed to be strangely warmed upon a reading of the rather slimy instructions in Leviticus for removing and burning the fat from the kidneys of goats? Was the sure and certain knowledge of inspiration to pervade one's being upon reading the blood-curdling butchery of Judges? Was I really to sense the peace that passes understanding descending in Shekinah glory upon my inmost being as I persevered through the gloating curses of Nahum or the reams of numbing census statistics in Numbers? If so, it wasn't happening. Yet I had indeed and in truth trusted Jesus as my Lord and Savior and still do.

Don't get me wrong. I did *not* conclude that these books were not authentic, inspired Scripture. What I *did* conclude was that the guidance of the Spirit was not to be equated with some mysterious "inner witness" in such matters.

Blind Alley #2: No Direct Witness to the Canon by Christ

So I turned away from my fitful and flickering inner light to the sure and certain witness of the Scriptures themselves. They should be the standard for judging this matter since, after all, Jesus had urged us to "search the Scriptures." Indeed, I sought out that specific verse in the hope that here I might find a clue. It read as follows:

> You search the Scriptures, because you think
> that in them you have eternal life; and it is they
> that bear witness to me (Jn 5:39 RSV).

That was it. Not a syllable hinting that Scripture was self-attesting, but instead the insistence that Scripture attested to *Christ*, who himself was rather vague as to what he meant by "Scripture." As I read further I noted that Christ spoke of "Moses and all the Prophets" (Lk 24:27), but he did not spell out what that *meant*. Did this include the deuterocanonical books like Baruch? Did he regard the Wisdom literature such as the Song of Songs as Scripture? I sought for some proof from the words of Christ that, say, 1 and 2 Chronicles were indubitably the word of God and that 1 and 2 Maccabees weren't. I found none.

Blind Alley #3: No Witness to the Canon by the Apostles

So I turned to the writings of the apostles, particularly those which had been commended to me as "proof texts" for the self-attestation of Scripture. Chief among them was the famous 2 Timothy 3:16-17, to which I turned in great hope for an answer. It reads:

> All Scripture is God-breathed and is useful for
> teaching, rebuking, correcting and training in
> righteousness, so that the man of God may be
> thoroughly equipped for every good work.

This was both wonderfully clear and utterly exasperating. For this passage, the closest Paul gets to talking about the Bible and its nature, is silent about the Bible's contents. What, precisely, *was* this God-breathed Scripture for Paul? Or Peter? Or John? Or Jude? Or James? They didn't say.

Blind Alley #4: Does Quotation Equal Canonicity?

"The answer to this puzzle," said my Evangelical friends, "is simple. What do Jesus and his apostles *quote*? Find that and you've found your answer to what is and isn't Scripture. Though they give no official list, still they quote from the truly inspired books of the Old Testament and studiously ignore the apocryphal books like Wisdom or 1 Maccabees. That's how you tell what has and hasn't got the seal of inspiration and canonicity." This seemed like a very promising solution to the riddle, so I checked it out to see if it was really so. What I discovered gave me a headache.

It is quite true that Jesus and the apostles refer to many books as Scripture. Isaiah, Psalms, Proverbs, Jeremiah, Genesis, Exodus, Deuteronomy, and others are frequently cited or alluded to with the prefaces like "It is written" or "Scripture says," so we can be certain that they regarded these books as inspired and commended them to us as such.

But Jesus and the apostles utterly *ignore* a lot of other books in the Old Testament. Consider Ecclesiastes, Esther, or the Song of Songs. None of them are mentioned or even alluded to in the New Testament. The exclusion of the Song of Songs is particularly odd since there are a number of places in the New Testament (like Paul's discourse on marriage in Ephesians 5) where it would surely seem to be useful to refer to the Song's glorious portrayal of married love and its wonderful uses as an image of Christ and the Church. Lots of subsequent Christian writers have used it for just this. Yet Paul ignores it. Why then (given the "quotation=canonicity" formula my friends had proposed) did we Evangelicals assume that the Song of Songs is canonical given such a pointed omission by both Jesus and the apostles in their discussions of marriage and of Christ and the Bride?

And that wasn't the worst of it! For I discovered that the apostles, in addition to ignoring books that are in the canon, also cite books that aren't! For instance, Jude tells the story of the Archangel Michael disputing with the devil over the body of Moses. Where in the Old Testament is this story? Nowhere. It is, rather, in the Assumption of Moses, a book so apocryphal it didn't even make it into the apocrypha![5] Likewise, Jude quotes the following and declares it to be "prophecy" (that is, divinely inspired):

> See, the Lord is coming with thousands upon thousands of his holy ones to judge everyone, and to convict all the ungodly of all the ungodly acts they have done in the ungodly way, and of all the harsh words ungodly sinners have spoken against him (Jude 14-15).

Where is this divinely inspired word found? Obadiah? Zephaniah? Judges? No. Perhaps 1 Chronicles, Ezra or Nehemiah then? Nope. Maybe it is in Lamentations or Nahum? Again no, for none of *these* Old Testament books are ever once quoted in the New Testament either. Yet the book from which this prophecy comes — Enoch — *is* quoted as inspired and yet is *not* in the canon of Scripture or even in the deuterocanonical books. Why not, if apostolic quotation equals canonicity?

Further, I realized that my friends' "quotation=canonicity" criterion was impossible to apply to some other quotes of Paul's. Paul quotes the pagan poet Menander saying, "Bad company corrupts good character" (1 Cor 15:33). He quotes Aratus, a third century B.C. pagan poet, speaking of human beings as God's creation: "We are his offspring" (Acts 17:28). He also quotes the pagan poet Epimenides, who wrote, "In him we live and move and have our being" (Acts 17:28). Most exasperating of all, Paul not only quotes Epimenides but goes so far as to call this pagan a *prophet*! (Ti 1:12).

By my friends' lights, it would appear then that Epimenides' writings ought to be inserted into the canon. Yet, of course, neither they nor I were ready to do that. The nagging question was "Why not?"

Blind Alley #5: Does Congruence with Other Scripture Equal Canonicity?

My Evangelical friends offered another suggestion. "It could be," they said, "that some books are to be regarded as inspired because they are congruent with the books that we *know* are inspired. So, for instance, Ezra and Nehemiah are inspired because they agree with the Big League Prophets like Haggai. Conversely, the apocryphal books wash out because they're not quoted *and* because they don't agree with the rest of Scripture."

So once again, I launched off, in hope that this would explain how the Scripture was self-attesting. But almost immediately I ran into more difficulties.

First was the problem of the many passages in the bona fide Old Testament that look a great deal (to me at any rate) like they conflicted mightily with the rest of Scripture, just as James, according to Luther, conflicted with Paul. For instance, I am not the only person to read Psalm 137 and notice an apparent discrepancy between the moral vision of the psalmist and that of the Sermon on the Mount. Our Lord says plainly, "Love your enemies, do good to those who hate you, bless those who curse you, pray for those who mistreat you" (Lk 6:27-28). But the psalmist says of his enemies:

> O Daughter of Babylon, doomed to destruction,
> happy is he who repays you
> for what you have done to us —
> he who seizes your infants
> and dashes them against the rocks (Ps 137:8-9).

This is but one of the so-called "cursing" psalms. Left to my own resources, I would never have concluded this is obviously reconcilable to the teachings of the gospels. Neither could I say that, left to myself, the various Old Testament accounts of divinely inspired genocide against the inhabitants of Canaan would have ever appeared remotely congruent with the Golden Rule.

"To you, perhaps they are not," said my friends, "But to Christ and the apostles they are, for they quote from and allude to books like Psalms and 1 Samuel frequently, despite their high body counts."

This was true, though, as the citations of Enoch and Epimenides showed, quotation doesn't necessarily equal canonicity. Moreover, I was still in a pickle. What about Old Testament books that are both ignored by the New Testament *and* incongruent with the rest of Scripture?

An outstanding example is Ecclesiastes. Given the twin criteria my friends had thus far suggested — citation in the New Testament and congruence with the rest of Scripture — how could I make any case for the self-attesting inspiration of this book? Ecclesiastes is totally ignored by the rest of Scripture and its nihilistic vision of life conflicts mightily with Christian hope. Why then do we regard as canonical a book (cited nowhere in the New Testament) that describes life as "vanity" and teaches that "the dead know nothing, they have no further reward" (Eccl 9:5)?

Apart from the fact that everyone *told* me Ecclesiastes is inspired and canonical, how was I supposed to reach such a wholly counter-intuitive conclusion about a book which seemed to flatly contradict the very essence of Christian hope in the fulfillment and resurrection promised by Christ?

Indeed, Ecclesiastes was a triple threat: no New Testament witness, no congruence with the rest of Scripture, and not so much as a flicker of the inner witness of the Spirit was discernible in my heart. So why should I believe it inspired and canonical?

Blind Alley #6: Begging the Question and Special Pleading

My friends tentatively suggested that "God inspired Ecclesiastes to show us what life was like without Him." Now this is an admirable theory and one to which I, in fact, now subscribe. But such a theory said *nothing* whatever about how an individual could determine the book's canonicity or inspiration. It only offered a helpful suggestion about what to do with the book once we knew what we had yet to prove: that Ecclesiastes is canonical and inspired.

Utterly unaddressed by this suggestion is the question of *why* I should regard Ecclesiastes as inspired in the first place if the New Testament never quotes it and it appears to flatly contradict the teaching of our Lord concerning the hope of the resurrection? If we move away from such direct question-begging and reply: "Well, the Scripture needs *some* sort of picture of godless despair to show us what life without Christ is like." I am forced to ask four questions in response:

1. Aren't there plenty of pictures of godlessness in Scripture already — Saul and Judas and the Pharisees, for example?

2. How do we *know* Scripture needs another such picture?

3. How do we know Ecclesiastes *is* that inspired picture?

4. If the criteria for determining the self-attestation of Scripture are quotation and congruence with the rest of Scripture, why are the arguments for Ecclesiastes' inspiration and canonicity not a spectacular case of special pleading? What's the difference between saying that we need Ecclesiastes because we need a portrait of godlessness and saying we need, say, 1 Maccabees because Scripture needs *some* sort of history of what happened after the time of Ezra?

I concluded that, left to my own resources, I would have never have seen Ecclesiastes as a scriptural book. Rather, I accepted it because I had been taught to by the church I belonged to.

The same goes for Esther. I was forced to admit I accepted

this book (which without its deuterocanonical additions, doesn't even mention God) not because my spirit had leapt up in joy at the taste of its self-attesting nature, but because someone (in fact, all of Christianity) told me, "This is the word of God," and I, trusting Christianity's word, had simply nodded assent.

When I questioned my Evangelical friends about this, they replied that Esther is canonical because it demonstrates the providence of God at work in the rescue of Israel from annihilation at the hands of Haman and in the establishment of the Feast of Purim. I replied that: 1) This again begs the question and that 2) you could say exactly the same thing about the deuterocanonical 1 and 2 Maccabees, with their thrilling tale of the rescue of Judaism from annihilation at the hands of Antiochus Epiphanes and the establishment of the Feast of Hanukkah. Yet, according to my friends, Esther somehow obviously attests itself to be a part of the inspired Scripture while the books of the Maccabees somehow obviously do not.

Why?

This was the same problem as Ecclesiastes, only worsened by a contrast with the apocrypha. On the one hand I had the canonical book of Esther which was not self-evidently anything besides a good story. It failed my friends' two tests of canonicity — quotation and congruence. It was neither mentioned in the New Testament nor, with its lack of interest in even bringing God into the story, was it particularly congruent with the rest of Scripture. In marked contrast to this was the far more congruent piety of the books of the Maccabees with their accounts of heroic acts done to the explicit glory of God. Moreover, 2 Maccabees 7 clearly teaches a faith in the afterlife and in resurrection which agrees quite well with the New Testament, yet stands out in sharp relief against the blank despair of Ecclesiastes.

So again it looked a lot like special pleading to say that Esther or Ecclesiastes are obviously canonical while the books of the Maccabees are not.

Blind Alley #7: The Myth of the Ignored Deuterocanonicals

So I was coming to the point where I had to admit I had no idea why (apart from the word of my church) the sixty-six books in my *New International Version Bible* (and only those sixty-six) were inspired and canonical. Mind you, I certainly wasn't ready to *deny* any of the sixty-six books were Scripture. But I certainly could no longer claim that I had any clear idea of how I as an individual could determine this simply by praying and reading my Bible.

Moreover, I was becoming even less confident about how to regard the so-called apocryphal or deuterocanonical books. For to my great surprise I discovered that, so far from being ignored in the New Testament like Ecclesiastes or Esther, deuterocanonical books *are* indeed quoted by, alluded to, and spookily congruent with the Scriptures acknowledged by us Evangelicals.

Consider, for instance, Wisdom 2:12-20 (written c. 100 B.C. and regarded by Catholic teaching as a prophecy of the Passion of Christ):

> Let us beset the just one, because he is obnoxious to us:
> he sets himself against our doings,
> Reproaches us for transgressions of the law
> and charges us with violations of our training.
> He professes to have a knowledge of God
> and styles himself a child of the Lord.
> To us he is the censure of our thoughts;
> merely to see him is a hardship for us,
> Because his life is not like other men's,
> and different are his ways.
> He judges us debased;
> he holds aloof from our paths as from things impure.
> He calls blest the destiny of the just

and boasts that God is his Father.
Let us see whether his words be true;
let us find out what will happen to him.
For if the just one be the son of God, he will
defend him
and deliver him from the hand of his foes.
With revilement and torture let us put him to
the test
that we may have proof of his gentleness
and try his patience.
Let us condemn him to a shameful death;
for according to his own words, God will take
care of him (NAB).

Compare this with Matthew's account of the crucifixion:

In the same way the chief priests, the teachers
of the law and the elders mocked him. "He
saved others," they said, "but he can't save
himself! He's the King of Israel! Let him come
now down from the cross, and we will believe
in him. He trusts in God. Let God rescue him
now if he wants him, for he said, 'I am the Son
of God' " (Mt 27:41-43).

Eerie, no? If quotation or allusion is what distinguishes a canonical book from a non-canonical one, then I would swear that all three synoptic gospel accounts of the crucifixion are making an obvious connection between this passage in Wisdom and the taunts of the mob at the foot of the Cross, thereby implying that Wisdom is Scripture. If quotation does not equal canonicity, I would still come away with the distinct impression that whoever wrote Wisdom either had a real stroke of luck in describing the fate of the "son of God" in a sinful world or else he was writing under the influence of something that looked remarkably like divine prophetic inspiration.

And this was not the only passage in the deuterocanonicals which dovetailed with the New Testament. Look at this passage from Wisdom 13:1 and 5 concerning the way Creation testifies to God's glory:

> For all men were by nature foolish who were
> in ignorance of God,
> and who from the good things seen did not suc-
> ceed in knowing him who is,
> and from studying the works did not discern
> the artisan. . . .
> For from the greatness and beauty of created
> things
> their original author, by analogy, is seen (NAB).

Try as I might, I could not deny that this sounded to me a great deal like Paul's statement that:

> What may be known about God is plain to
> them, because God has made it plain to them.
> For since the creation of the world God's in-
> visible qualities — his eternal power and di-
> vine nature — have been clearly seen, being
> understood from what has been made, so that
> men are without excuse (Rom 1:19-20).

Likewise, Wisdom's indictment of the idolatry of the pagans:

> For they went are astray in the paths of error,
> taking for gods the worthless and disgusting
> among beasts,
> deceived like senseless infants.
> Therefore as through upon unreasoning children,
> you sent your judgment on them as a mockery
> (Wis 12:24-25 NAB).

sounds a whole lot like Paul's thinking concerning the same matter:

> Therefore God gave them over in the sinful desire of their hearts to sexual impurity for the degrading of their bodies with one another. They exchanged the truth of God for a lie, and worshiped and served created things rather than the Creator — who is forever praised (Rom 1:24-25).

Then, there is Sirach 27:6:

> The fruit of a tree shows the care it has had; so too does a man's speech disclose the bent of his mind (NAB).

and our Lord's words:

> Every good tree bears good fruit, but a bad tree bears bad fruit. A good tree cannot bear bad fruit, and a bad tree cannot bear good fruit. Every tree that does not bear good fruit is cut down and thrown in to the fire. Thus, by their fruit you will recognize them (Mt 7:17-20).

Or again, notice Jesus observing Hanukkah (Jn 10:22-36), the establishment of which is recorded in the supposedly uninspired and non-canonical books of the Maccabees. Note especially his words spoken on the occasion of this feast:

> Jesus answered them, "Is it not written in your Law, 'I have said you are gods'? If he called them 'gods,' to whom the word of God came — and the Scripture cannot be broken — what

about the one whom the Father set apart as his
very own and sent into the world?" (Jn 10:34-
36).

This quote is significant because Jesus, standing near the
Temple during the Feast of Hanukkah, speaks of his being
"set apart" just as Judas Maccabeus "set apart" the Temple
in 1 Maccabees 4:36-59 and 2 Maccabees 10:1-8. He makes
a connection that would have been unmistakable to a Jewish
hearer: treating the Feast of Hanukkah and the account of it
in the books of the Maccabees as an image or type of his
own consecration by the Father. That is, he treats the Feast
of Hanukkah from the "apocryphal" book of Maccabees
exactly as he treats scriptural accounts of the manna (Jn
6:32-33; Ex 16:4), the Bronze Serpent (Jn 3:14; Num 21:4-
9), and Jacob's Ladder (Jn 1:51; Gen 28:12) — as an inspired prophetic image of Himself.

That made at least four deuterocanonical books — 1 and 2
Maccabees, Sirach, and Wisdom — looking a great deal as
though Christ and the apostles regarded them as Scripture. Yet
we Evangelicals had said their acceptance was an unbiblical
blunder of the early Church rectified by the Reformation. Which
immediately raised a question.

Blind Alley #8: No Certainty That Rejected Books Are Not Canonical

If the deuterocanonical books *were* mistakenly accepted
as inspired by the early Church, why was the failure to canonize the Gospel of Thomas or the book of Enoch *not* a mistake as well? This is, after all, the basis of the whole modernist attack on Scripture — that mistakes were made in assem-
bling the canon. If I thought the early Church messed up by
hailing Tobit as inspired Scripture, how could I be certain
that it had not also messed up in *rejecting*, say, Clement's
letter to the Corinthians?

And how was I to ever resolve the question on my own?

Blind Alley #9: No Certainty About the New Testament Canon Based on Scripture Alone

This deepening confusion didn't get any easier when I turned to the question of the New Testament canon. I recalled that Josh McDowell had argued that the motto of the early Church in canonizing Scripture was "If in doubt, throw it out."[6] According to McDowell, the Church was dubious about canonizing anything without direct apostolic authority behind it. Thus, we have apostolic writings from John, Matthew, Peter, and Paul and writings from their friends Luke (behind whom Paul stands) and Mark (behind whom Peter stands).

Yet, two big problems arise if we accept McDowell's logic. First, on this basis, a strong argument can be made for the canonicity of Clement's letter to the Corinthians. For Clement seems to be as much a member of the circle of apostolic disciples as Luke and Mark were. He is writing about 80 A.D., during the very lifetime of the Apostle John.[7] Indeed, Clement (who may be the very same Clement that Paul commends as a "fellow worker" in Philippians 4:3) is clearly regarded by the early Church as having an authority derived from the apostles just as the Evangelists do. Irenaeus (c. 180), tells us Clement "had seen the blessed Apostles and was acquainted with them." With those kind of credentials it is therefore not surprising that, in his letter to the Corinthians, Clement speaks with the assumption that Christians halfway across the Mediterranean will recognize his authority over them. Nor is it odd that his letters are treasured, preserved, and circulated by the Corinthian church to which he wrote, just as Paul's were. So why then are Luke and Mark canonized while Clement's letter to the Corinthians is not?

If we reply that we shouldn't canonize Clement based on the testimony of some second-century guy like Irenaeus, this faces us with our second problem: namely, that it is *only* because of second-, third-, and fourth-century guys like Irenaeus, Papias, Eusebius, and various others that we have any documentary evidence whatsoever that Mark and Luke wrote the gospels attributed to them. Thus, to reject this testimony about Clement is to confront the question of how we are supposed to assess the authorship of those books which *are* canonical. After all, not one of the gospels is signed. Therefore, on the basis of Scripture alone I had no reason at all to say that they are from Matthew, Mark, Luke, or John, much less inspired and canonical. All we have to accredit the apostolic origins of these books is the testimony of these second-, third-, and fourth-century guys, as the Jesus Seminar had pointed out. Or take 2 Peter. Why, on the basis of the text alone, should we take the author's word for it that he is Peter or even expressive of Petrine thought? Because he says so? The Gospel of Thomas and the Protevangelium of James likewise claim apostolic authorship. How was a layman like me to decide which is apostolic and which is bogus on the basis of the text alone? By the witness of my spirit? What if (as is the case) my personal sense of the anointing or congruence of the text rejected not only Thomas but Revelation as well? What if my spirit did not witness to the passages on hell in the canonical gospels or on predestination in Romans either?

I had been through all this with the Old Testament. I was coming back to a notion that I had already rejected — that we discern the canonicity of Scripture via some subjective and illusory "inner witness." I therefore flung myself one last time into a search for the self-attestation of Scripture. In a sort of shriveled desperation, I tried one last time to see if perhaps the New Testament could give some sense of what did and did not belong in the New Testament.

But this last gasp effort only succeeded in confronting me with the most puzzling conundrum of all: the letter to the Hebrews. Why is *this* book called canonical Scripture at all, especially by Josh McDowell or an Evangelical like me? After all, it is an anonymous book that, unlike the gospels, did not even have unanimous endorsement in the early Church.[8] To be sure, some Fathers do endorse the book as apostolic and the consensus eventually tilts in its favor — after a couple of centuries. But there's a huge gulf between the early Church's tentative assessment that "This *may* just possibly be apostolic" and "If in doubt, throw it out." How then was Hebrews supposed to be self-attesting? What distinguished Hebrews from the equally anonymous (and equally ancient) Didache that rendered the former obviously inspired and the latter obviously not? Especially since Hebrews contained statements which, to my mind, were not readily congruent with the rest of Scripture, most notably the quotation of 2 Samuel 7:14 as a witness to Christ ("I will be his father, and he will be my son.") coupled with the assertion by the author that God made Jesus "perfect through suffering" (Heb 1:5; 2:10). If this were not in a book we already called Scripture, I would have had a tough time squaring that with the canonical gospel claims that Christ was eternally God's Son and was perfect *before* he suffered. Does it not give the strong appearance that the author believes there was a time when Jesus was both not the Son of God and not perfect?

Not only that, just to make things more confusing for me, Hebrews also alludes to the deuterocanonical books when it speaks of the suffering saints of the Old Covenant. Note, for instance, the following:

> Women received back their dead, raised to life again. Others were tortured and refused to be released, so that they might gain a better resurrection (Heb 11:35).

The people referred to in the first sentence are obvious. Both the Widow of Zarephath and the Shunammite "received back their dead," raised to life by Elijah and Elisha (1 Kgs 17:17-23; 2 Kgs 4:17-37). But who are these "others" who were "tortured and would not accept deliverance, in order to obtain a better resurrection?" There's only one place we can find such a story: 2 Maccabees 7, right in the middle of what I still (for reasons which were fuzzier all the time) called the apocrypha. This writing (and no other in the Old Testament period) fits the bill as it recounts the story of a mother and seven sons who undergo horrific tortures for the faith and who do so in the explicitly stated hope of the resurrection.

So how was I, a mere mortal, to fathom the canonicity of Hebrews given all this kaleidoscopic data?

The Way Out of the Blind Alleys

My one good fortune was that I am not a betting man. Thus, though I was confused about how I, as an individual, could know what was and wasn't Scripture, I was by no means prepared to start redefining the canon based on my ignorance and confusion. After all, I reasoned, the canon of Scripture had survived in relatively good shape for two thousand years, give or take a few deuterocanonicals. The glue which bound the canon together, though invisible to my eye, seemed to work tolerably well. Yet the visible thing, the thing I thought as plain as a pikestaff, was the one thing I certainly knew now did *not* work: the mirage of the self-attesting Bible.

Therefore, I realized, one of two things necessarily followed: either, as modernism said, the canon of Scripture *was* a merely human tradition or else *God must have ordained some sort of revelation outside of Scripture as the means by which we could know what Scripture was.* There was no third option.

The first option didn't hold up. Modernism's claim that Scripture is a human tradition still suffered a gross flaw: it still offered a preposterous scenario to replace the plain old gospel. The modernist theory of the "charismatic, mesmerizing, profoundly inspiring" (and utterly forgotten) "real Jesus" was simply silly. Such a Jesus was scarcely able to inspire a yawn, much less the idolatry of deluded apostles.

Which left me with the second option. So, to my surprise, I found myself asking a question I had never considered before:

What if Scripture alone *isn't* the sole source of revelation?

Notes

1. Martin Luther, *Preface to James' Epistle* in *Luther's Works*, Vol. 35, Helmut Lehmann, General Editor (Philadelphia: Muhlenberg Press, 1960), pp. 395-396.

2. *Preface to James' Epistle* in *Luther's Works*, Vol. 35, pp. 395-396.

3. *Preface to James' Epistle* in *Luther's Works*, Vol. 35, p. 397. Some have claimed that Luther changed his mind about James' canonicity later on. However, editions of the *Preface to James' Epistle* after 1530 read from this point, "Therefore I cannot include him among the chief books, though I would not thereby prevent anyone from including him or extolling him as he pleases, for there are otherwise many good sayings in him." In other words, after 1530 Luther still thinks James is a nice book as Sirach is a nice book, but his rejection of James from the New Testament, though somewhat muted, remains in force.

4. *Preface to the New Testament* in *Luther's Works*, Vol. 35, p. 362.

5. *The Jerome Biblical Commentary*, Vol. 2, Raymond E. Brown, S.S., Joseph A. Fitzmeyer, S.J., Roland E. Murphy, O. Carm., eds. (Englewood Cliffs: Prentice-Hall, 1968), p. 379.

6. Josh McDowell, *Evidence That Demands a Verdict*, Vol. 1 (San Bernardino: Here's Life Publishers, 1979), p. 29.

7. William Jurgens (*The Faith of the Early Fathers*, Vol. 1 [Collegeville: The Liturgical Press, 1970], pp. 6-7) argues cogently and, I think, conclusively, for this date.

8. Hebrews (like several other New Testament books) shows very dubious evidence that it was particularly self-attesting to the Christians of the earliest centuries. Thus, Irenaeus excludes Hebrews, 2 Peter, and 3 John from the canon. The Muratorian canon excludes Hebrews, James, 1 and 2 Peter, and 3 John. Eusebius disputes James, 2 Peter, 2 and 3 John,

and Jude. The Syrian Church and many eastern Fathers reject Revelation (sources: *New Bible Dictionary*, 2nd Edition, J.D. Douglas, Organizing Editor [Wheaton: Tyndale House, 1984], p. 173; *The Jerome Biblical Commentary*, Vol. 2, Raymond E. Brown, S.S., Joseph A. Fitzmeyer, S.J., Roland E. Murphy, O. Carm., eds. [Englewood Cliffs: Prentice-Hall, 1968], p. 468).

CHAPTER FIVE
THE DOG THAT
DIDN'T BARK

*How often have I said to you that when you have eliminated
the impossible, whatever remains, however improbable,
must be the truth? — Sherlock Holmes*

I felt it was scandalous to even ask such a thing, yet I could not see how to avoid asking it. So I went back to square one and contemplated the question with which this inquiry had begun: "Why is the canon of Scripture not the tradition of men?"

I had focused on one word in that question during my last go-around: "canon." As a result, I was now certain of one thing: the "self-attesting canon" hypothesis did not hold up under scrutiny. What I was *not* certain of was modernism's proposition: "Therefore orthodox Christianity is wrong." Thus, though I was personally unsure about the canon of Scripture, I didn't see any particular reason why I couldn't treat the biblical books as documents which the Church, at any rate, regarded as fixed and authoritative, till I got my own questions ironed out.

So I decided to reread the riddle and see what happened if I focused on another word this time. What if I searched the Scripture to find out what it said about *tradition*? Such a search might at least give me more clues to work with than the myth of the "self-attesting" Scripture.

I whipped out my trusty concordance and looked up words

like "tradition" and "teachings" . . . that sort of thing. As I expected, there were the usual suspects: the quotes from Jesus and the apostles which I already knew, warning against trusting in the traditions of men. But in addition to these, I noticed something else.

Paul twice *commands* and *commends* adherence to tradition! I blinked and looked again. It was still there. First, he tells the Thessalonians:

> So then, brethren, stand firm and hold to the traditions which you were taught by us, either by word of mouth or by letter (2 Thes 2:15 RSV).

In plain Greek, Paul says "Hold to the *paradosis* which you were taught by us, either by word of mouth [that is, by extra-biblical oral teaching] or by letter [that is, by epistles like 2 Thessalonians]." This caught me off guard, but it could not be denied. Paul not only commands an adherence to tradition, he expressly warns his readers to shun anybody who doesn't.

> Now we command you, brethren, in the name of our Lord Jesus Christ, that you keep away from any brother who is living in idleness and not in accord with the tradition that you received from us (2 Thes 3:6 RSV).

Again, the word was *paradosis* or "tradition" and referred not merely to Paul's writings but to the word he had orally delivered to the Thessalonians when he was with them.

So there I was, timidly creeping through Scripture, wondering if I might possibly reconcile a little extra-biblical revelation with the Bible when Paul himself appears, suddenly slapping me on the back and loudly *demanding* that I not only reconcile it, but obey it as nothing less than an apostolic commandment!

This was quite disorienting and made me cautious lest I make a misstep. So I started asking around again about what a Bible-centered guy like me ought to do about these verses. What was this mysterious tradition of which Paul spoke and to which I was supposed to hold fast?

My Evangelical friends said, "That's easy. The Scriptures." They told me that since, of course, the New Testament had not yet been written (the letters to the Thessalonians are some of the earliest in the New Testament) it was necessary for the Church to rely on the oral teaching of the apostles until the Bible was complete. Once the Bible *was* complete, it said everything that had constituted the *paradosis* Paul mentions. So apostolic "tradition" means, for us, Scripture and only Scripture. The *New Bible Dictionary* explained it this way:

> Apostolic tradition was at one time oral, but for us it is crystallized in the apostolic writing containing the Spirit-guided witness to the Christ of God. Other teaching, while it may be instructive and useful and worthy of serious consideration, cannot claim to be placed alongside the Old Testament and New Testament as authoritative without manifesting the same defect as condemned Jewish tradition in the eyes of our Lord.[1]

"So," said my friends, "the whole matter can be summed up in the words of Paul himself, 'When perfection comes, the imperfect disappears' (1 Cor 13:10). When Scripture came, it swallowed up the *paradosis* of which Paul spoke so that there is no revelation passed on to us anywhere but in Scripture."

Now, my friends (and the *New Bible Dictionary*) stated all this as fact, just as though we somehow *knew* it to be true. Yet as I began to think about these things for the first time, it occurred to me that our basis in the biblical text for the "Scripture swallows tradition" doctrine was extremely hard to see. For as I continued to study the Bible I discovered I could not find the slightest hint in 2 Thessalonians or anywhere else that the *paradosis* of which Paul spoke would someday, in Paul's game plan of revelation, be "crystallized" in Scripture alone. On the contrary, one of the odd things about Paul's command in 2 Thessalonians 2:15 was that he seemed to regard the tradition he had given them as *not* being in any special need of "crystallization." Although he clearly regards his writings as invested with apostolic authority and therefore as the word of God (1 Thes 2:13), Paul nonetheless speaks, not of some future complete New Testament as the one and only source of revelation, but of "the teaching you received from us" — a teaching which was almost entirely oral and which 1 and 2 Thessalonians seem to be written to buttress, not replace. Thus, in contrast to my friends and the *New Bible Dictionary*, it looked for all the world to me as though Paul refers the Thessalonians to the oral *paradosis* of the *past*, not to the completed canon of the future; to what they have already *heard*, not merely to what he is now putting down on papyrus.

This seems to be the general attitude of all the New Testament writers. Luke, for instance, also writes his gospel to buttress, not swallow, the oral tradition Theophilus had already received. As Luke himself says, "It seemed good also to me to write an orderly account for you, most excellent Theophilus, so that you may know the certainty of the things you have been taught [that is, the oral *paradosis*]" (Lk 1:3-4). In other words, Luke also appears to offer his writing in union with, not in replacement of, the tradition Theophilus has received. He too seems to think that Theophilus should hold fast to the traditions that he was taught, either by word of mouth or by letter.

So too, John is explicit in twice acknowledging that his mention of specific stories and teachings of Jesus is not meant to deny other extra-biblical traditions (Jn 20:30; 21:25), so long as these traditions do not oppose his teaching and that of the other apostles (1 Jn 2:18-19; 4:1-3; 2 Jn 7-9). For John, as for Paul and Luke, the litmus test for authentic Christian teaching is not "Is this written?" but "Is this apostolic?"

Thus, I could not find *any* testimony in the length and breadth of the New Testament documents that the apostolic *paradosis* was destined to be *wholly* committed to writing. Not from our Lord (who, though literate, never wrote a syllable of Scripture) nor from the Twelve (whom he never commanded to commit *anything* — much less *everything* — to writing, save the book of Revelation [Rv 1:19]), nor from any other non-apostolic author such as Luke, Mark, or the writer of Hebrews. Nowhere could I see a single shred of New Testament support for one of the central things we Evangelicals asserted: that the biblical writings crystallized the entirety of apostolic tradition.

Then a second thought occurred to me. "Just how," I wondered, "do we Evangelicals know what the content of these unwritten traditions was, since Paul did not spell them out in 2 Thessalonians?"

In essence, I had before me an open box called "*paradosis* handed on by letter" and a sealed box called "*paradosis* handed on by word of mouth." Paul did not spell out in 2 Thessalonians what was in the sealed box and so I did not know in the slightest what it may contain. Yet if I did not know, how did we Evangelicals know (and know with such certainty) that the contents of Box 1 (the complete Bible) and Box 2 (the pre-biblical tradition) were absolutely identical? The answer was, "We don't."

This led to the most puzzling question of all: namely, what did we mean when we tossed out a phrase like "once the Bible was complete?" Such words assumed precisely what I was trying to understand: the glaring question of the canon. How did we *know* its complete contents from Scripture alone? As we have seen, the answer is: we didn't and couldn't. Yet this phrase "once the Bible was complete" was the track on which the "Scripture swallowed tradition" argument traveled in a perfect circle. In plain English, we were saying, "We know Scripture is the totality of revelation because we know the totality of revelation is Scripture."

Yet I, at any rate, knew nothing of the sort. Nor, when I

pressed them, did my friends. For all our good intentions, it was becoming clear to me that our Evangelical assertion of the "self-attesting" Bible was dissolving into mere question-begging and was proving to be a sorry weapon in a contest with the faith-destroying logic of modernism.

Where had I gone wrong?

I reviewed the central contradiction I had discovered. None of us Evangelicals were willing to call the Bible's table of contents authoritative revelation. Yet for us to say "the Bible is complete" at all, we *had* to assume the table of contents carried divine authority; that *this* list of these books (and no other) was absolutely binding on every faithful believer. But to say *that* was to acknowledge that an extra-biblical tradition — call it the Tradition of the Table of Contents — was ... what? Merely "instructive and useful and worthy of serious consideration"? A human whim "manifesting the same defect as condemned Jewish tradition in the eyes of our Lord"? A negotiable item modernism could fiddle with under the cloak of the "liberty of the believer"? A piece of mere custom which might just as well exclude the Song of Songs and include the Gospel of Thomas if the believer felt like it?

Hardly! As I well knew, the canon of Scripture is regarded as absolutely nonnegotiable by Evangelicals. It is, in fact, treated exactly like revelation (and binding upon us, just as Paul insisted in 2 Thessalonians 2:15 concerning his extra-biblical teachings). So here, at least, there appeared to be not only a revealed, authoritative tradition which existed outside Scripture, *but a tradition even we Evangelicals regarded as binding upon ourselves!* Seeing this, and seeing that Scripture is silent about "swallowing tradition," *and* seeing that modernism was as persistent as ever in its desire to dismantle Christianity precisely by attacking the tradition of the canon, I decided I would see if perhaps Scripture had more to say concerning tradition than I had thought. When I did, I found the following clues.

Clue #1: The Old Testament Relies on Extra-biblical Tradition

The first thing I noticed when I started searching the Old Testament was that the writers never seemed to assume what we Evangelicals assume — that extra-biblical tradition is inherently dangerous and unreliable. Their implicit attitude on this point struck me as remarkable and oddly significant — like the dog that didn't bark in the Sherlock Holmes story. It is not so much that the Old Testament writers actively endorsed extra-biblical (or in this case, pre-biblical) tradition as revelation; it was just that it never occurred to them to question it and it *did* occur to them to assume it — thousands of years of it.

Consider that the first three covenants the Pentateuch relates — the Adamic, Noahic, and Abrahamic covenants — are all passed on orally, not only from God to Adam, Noah, and Abraham, but from them to their descendants. Adam and his descendants don't write a lick of Scripture, nor do any of the patriarchs. Indeed, we have no indication that much of anything that eventually got put into Genesis makes it into writing till at least the time of Moses, centuries after Abraham. Yet when God reveals himself to Moses, he speaks with the assumption that Moses will know who God is talking about when he declares, "I am the God of your father, the God of Abraham, the God of Isaac and the God of Jacob" (Ex 3:6). How does Moses know about these venerable old gentlemen (and about everything else in Genesis)?

"Because the Holy Spirit directly inspired Moses to know it," ventured some of my more robustly anti-tradition friends. Perhaps. But then he also seems to have inspired the entire Hebrew people on this point as well, since a few verses later we find Moses commissioned to pass these words of God on to them, also with the clear assumption that they too know just who Abraham, Isaac, and Jacob are (Ex 3:16). So unless we are prepared to believe that the entire contents of the book of Genesis were directly infused into the brains of all Israelites as well we must, I think, acknowledge that the stories preserved in Genesis were quite obviously passed down via oral tradition and preserved by the Holy Spirit in this manner just as they were later preserved by him in Scripture.

"Ah! But there you are!" said my friends, "The Holy Spirit's divinely revealed truths were, as you say, 'later preserved by him in Scripture,' not in Scripture and tradition. It is a biblical pattern that the message of God is never trusted to the shifting winds of mere tradition. It always gets written down and tradition then withers up and blows away. That's just a fact. And it's exactly why Christ and the apostles always say 'It is written' and why they never say 'it is said' or 'it is in our tradition that. . . . .' When they spoke of revelation they spoke of Scripture. Period."

Now it seemed to me that this was a strong (and strongly coherent) assertion. It had my gut sympathy too. After all, you don't find tradition handed down side by side with the books of Genesis, Exodus, or Isaiah, do you?

Or do you?

Clue #2: The New Testament Writers Rely on Extra-biblical Tradition

To my surprise, I discovered several passages in the New Testament that indeed rely upon tradition as the bearer of genuine, grade A revelation.

Consider, for example, the following statement made by Stephen just minutes before he was martyred. Speaking to the Jews of Jerusalem, he cries out, "And now you have betrayed and murdered him — you who have received the law that was put into effect through angels but have not obeyed it" (Acts 7:52-53).

Similarly, Paul declares to the Galatians, "The law was put into effect through angels" (Gal 3:19).

Yet a third New Testament writer, the author of Hebrews, concurs with Paul and Stephen, comparing the Mosaic Covenant with the New Covenant of Christ and warning, "For if the message spoken by angels was binding, and every violation and disobedience received its just punishment, how shall we escape if we ignore such a great salvation?" (Heb 2:2-3).

So here are three separate New Testament writers all bearing witness to the same teaching: that the Mosaic covenant was given to Moses, not directly from God, but via angelic mediation. Yet as I read this I was puzzled. I could remember nothing in Exodus or in any other Old Testament book about the Law being given through angels.

As I researched the question I discovered the reason for my failure to recall the Old Testament reference: there is none. Yet all three New Testament writers insist on the truth of this teaching nonetheless. Where then do they get their notion? From extra-biblical tradition, an extra-biblical tradition known, not only to these writers, but to other Jews as well.[2] Moreover, both Paul and the author of Hebrews make this tradition one of the underpinnings for their teaching that the covenant of Moses is inferior to the covenant of Christ, since the former was made through mere angelic creatures while the latter is made by the incarnate God himself!

This is not the only such instance of the New Testament treating tradition as revelation. Paul, for instance, also writes to Timothy this warning about deceivers in the Church and takes as his illustration an Old Testament incident:

> Just as Jannes and Jambres opposed Moses,
> so also these men oppose the truth — men of
> depraved minds, who, as far as the faith is con-
> cerned, are rejected. But they will not get very
> far because, as in the case of those men, their
> folly will be clear to everyone (2 Tm 3:8-9).

Consult your concordance. You will not find Jannes and Jambres anywhere in the Old Testament. But if you check out some handy Bible reference book you will find that Jannes and Jambres are the names of the Egyptian magicians who opposed Moses.

So the question arises: how does Paul know the names of these guys? Did he have a *very* early advance copy of the *New Bible Dictionary*? If we propose the "Paul was directly inspired" theory again, we have to ask, "Why then does Paul know that *Timothy* will know who he means?" After all, Paul gives no clue who Jannes and Jambres are other than that they opposed Moses. Lots of people opposed Moses. So Jannes and Jambres might be two of the nameless Israelites who periodically squawked at the Lawgiver. Yet it is obvious from the way Paul tosses off the names that both he and Timothy know who Jannes and Jambres are.

In fact, the *New Bible Dictionary* tells us that *lots* of their contemporaries knew.[3] For in fact, Paul is again drawing on (and assuming Timothy will draw on) a widely known *tradition* and treating it as authoritative revelation, even though it is extra-biblical. In short, Paul is again getting some of his revelation about Moses the same way Moses got some of his revelation about Abraham, Isaac, and Jacob — by an extra-biblical tradition.

Nor is Paul is the only one. Jude, as we observed in the last chapter, refers us to a prophecy of Enoch which is recorded nowhere in the Old Testament. How does he know of it? From the book of Enoch, a rather late piece of work dating from the century or two before Christ. But here's the catch: Enoch lived considerably before that. Indeed Enoch was born a considerable stretch of years before *Noah*. Thus for Jude to quote a prophecy of Enoch's as inspired revelation is Jude's acknowledgment that tradition — in this case the tradition of Enoch's prophecy — is revelatory.

Likewise, Jude also makes reference to the odd incident of the Archangel Michael disputing with Satan over the body of Moses. As we noted in the last chapter, this too is a tradition found nowhere in the Old Testament, but it is preserved in the Assumption of Moses. Evidently both Jude and the author of the Assumption regard this extra-biblical tradition as important.

Finally, we find that the epistle to the Hebrews looks a great deal as though it too is drawing on tradition. For the author writes concerning the prophets who suffered in hope of the coming redemption:

> Some faced jeers and flogging, while still others were chained and put in prison. They were stoned; they were sawed in two; they were put to death by the sword (Heb 11:36).

Now although we find many Old Testament saints facing jeers, flogging, and the sword, nowhere in the Old Testament do we find reference to any hero or prophet martyred by being sawn in two. Where then does the author of Hebrews get this notion?

It comes from the Ascension of Isaiah 5:1-14, another piece of late Old Testament-era literature which was never canonized.[4] It records the tradition that Isaiah met his end this way.

Now the book of Enoch, the Assumption of Moses, and the Ascension of Isaiah are all books which nobody — Protestant, Catholic, Orthodox, or Jew — calls inspired Scripture. This had been a puzzle as long as I had been laboring under the illusion that New Testament quotation of a book guarantees its canonicity. But then something occurred to me. Suppose these books are just regular, old, uninspired, and non-canonical books — the Old Testament equivalent of a sci-fi novel. Does that automatically mean they cannot incorporate into their fantastic little tales some real truth culled from authentic tradition, just as Paul did in culling Jannes' and Jambres' names from tradition? After all, I could write a science fiction story about time travel and center it around an attempt to prevent President Kennedy from dying in Dallas on November 22, 1963. Yet the fact that my book is fantasy doesn't change the fact that JFK died by assassination at that time and place. Similarly, the writer of Enoch could (and apparently did, according to Jude) preserve a real tradition and set it in the midst of an otherwise ordinary human work — a tradition of which he and Jude are both aware, just as you and I are both aware of how and when President Kennedy died. The same is true for the tradition recorded in the Assumption of Moses and the Ascension of Isaiah and cited by Jude and Hebrews. In short, the biblical writers seem to have gotten their information about God and his world as Paul said they should: by tradition, both written and unwritten.

Clue #3: Jesus Relies on Tradition

So now I had not only my own Evangelical heritage acting as though the tradition of the canon was revelatory, I also had both Old and New Testament writers acting the same way about other aspects of tradition. What, I wondered, did Jesus say about all this?

I thought I knew, what with all those "Woe to yous" he directed against the Pharisees and their traditions. But I'd been seriously mistaken about a lot of other things, so I went back to the gospels to see if I could make sense of this apparent contradiction. Perhaps something in our Lord's words could untangle the apparent disagreement between his warnings about tradition and the practice of the biblical writers.

Something did, and ironically it was his teaching about the Pharisees that crowned it all. For he tells his disciples:

> The teachers of the law and the Pharisees sit in Moses' seat. So you must obey them and do everything they tell you. But do not do what they do, for they do not practice what they preach (Mt 23:2-3).

The irony is that nowhere in the Old Testament do we find reference to "Moses' seat" as the symbol for the teaching authority in Israel. Where then is the term found? In tradition![5] Yet Jesus not only recognizes such a position of authority and calls it by its traditional name, he lays great stress on it and binds his followers to honor it (in fact, to honor it *more* than the unworthy men who occupy that seat). He too acts just the way Paul says we should act: he honors authentic *paradosis* whether it comes via word of mouth or by Scripture.

Hmmmmm. It was slowly beginning to dawn on me that my view of tradition had been seriously lopsided. Scripture condemned tradition at times; but that's not the only thing it said about tradition. From our Lord to the New Testament writers, from the Old Testament heroes to my contemporary Catholic acquaintances — indeed, even my Evangelical friends and me with our implicit acceptance of the Tradition of the Table of Contents — I was startled to find that *some* sort of authoritative tradition seemed to be woven side by side with Scripture all through the Christian revelation. In fact, the more I looked at it, the more inseparable the Scripture and *paradosis* seemed to become.

"Of course," said my Evangelical friends. "As we have said all along, Scripture and nothing else *is* the *paradosis*. That is exactly why it was canonized: to make it the final rule of faith by which all extra-biblical tradition is judged.

"That is why we Evangelicals are able to rely on Scripture alone as the source of all our Christian beliefs, speaking forth only what Scripture speaks, keeping silent where Scripture is silent, and not binding the conscience of the believer to tradition (as the Catholic Church does) on questions in which Scripture is ambiguous. For us, extra-biblical tradition, however useful it may be, is just not revelation."

Which got me thinking.

Notes

1. *New Bible Dictionary*, 2nd Edition, J.D. Douglas, Organizing Editor (Wheaton: Tyndale House, 1984), p. 1212.
2. *The Jerome Biblical Commentary*, Vol. 2, Raymond E. Brown, S.S., Joseph A. Fitzmeyer, S.J., Roland E. Murphy, O. Carm., eds. (Englewood Cliffs: Prentice-Hall, 1968), p.

243. (According to this commentary this tradition is attested, not only by these New Testament writers, but by such sources as Josephus' *Antiquities of the Jews* and the *Book of Jubilees*.)

3. *New Bible Dictionary*, p. 551.
4. *The Jerome Biblical Commentary*, Vol. 2, p. 402.
5. *The Jerome Biblical Commentary*, Vol. 2, p. 102.

CHAPTER SIX
THE LENS IN MY EYE

When you are reading a book it is obvious (once you attend to it) that you are using your eyes: but unless your eyes begin to hurt you, or the book is a text book on optics, you may read all evening without once thinking of eyes. — C.S. Lewis[1]

I wondered: is it really true that we Evangelicals never treat extra-biblical tradition as authoritative revelation? Is it really the case that *all* Evangelical belief is derived from the clear and unambiguous teaching of the Bible alone? Do we *really* speak forth only what Scripture speaks, keep silent where Scripture is silent, and never bind the conscience of the believer on those questions in which Scripture permits different interpretations?

I wondered. Especially since the living fossil of the Tradition of the Table of Contents still inexplicably swam like a coelacanth in the ocean of Evangelical faith precisely where we said tradition had gone extinct. What if there were *other* supposedly extinct extra-biblical coelacanths down there too?

To find out, I decided to try an experiment. I would look at Evangelical — not Catholic — belief and practice to see if there was any other evidence of tradition being treated like revelation. I would see if there were any other rock-bottom, non-negotiable, grade A, can't-do-without-'em beliefs which, like the Table of Contents, were not attested (or very weakly attested) in the Bible, yet which we orthodox Evangelicals treated like revelation. If I found such things, and if they had an ancient pedigree, it seemed to me this would be very strong evidence that the apostolic *paradosis* not only *was* larger than the Bible alone, but that it had — somehow — been handed down to the present.

So I started taking a good long look at non-negotiable Evangelical beliefs as they were actually lived out in my church and churches like it. To my surprise, I found several such weakly attested non-negotiables.

The Sanctity of Human Life

Arguably the most pressing issue of our time is the question of the sanctity of human life from conception to natural death. While you are reading this book, several thousand preborn babies, ranging in age from first trimester to full term, are going to be safely, cleanly, and legally suctioned, burnt, dismembered, or decapitated by skilled professionals who collect large paychecks, walk their dogs, drink soda pop, and appear to the naked eye as ordinary human beings. As this evil occurs, a bewildered modern society, long ago cut adrift from its Christian roots, will not recoil in horror but will instead flop its hands passively in its lap, register a fuddled shrug of discomfort, and continue lacking the capacity to tell whether or not this is bad. Occasionally, when it is in the mood for righteous indignation, it will watch a Holocaust documentary on cable TV and shake its head at how the people of Germany could have permitted such things.

Meanwhile, the culture of death will not sleep. Rather, emboldened by our moral paralysis in the face of so obvious an evil, the purveyors of "choice" will ask ever more loudly, "If we can do these things when the tree is green, what can we get away with when it is dry? If the life of the helpless infant is cheap when the economy is strong, why not the life of the disabled, aged, and sick when medical costs skyrocket?"

So as acquiescence to abortion proceeds apace, thousands

of other apparently ordinary people are working day and night — and with steadily growing success — to acquire the right for "qualified medical professionals" to kill innocent human beings whose lives are "unworthy of being lived." They live for Dr. Jack Kevorkian's dream of "Medicide Clinics," where "patients" can be killed by means of "physician-assisted suicide." To that end, initiatives and court cases proliferate across the country seeking to grant, not the "right to die" (we already have that) but the power of doctors (and eventually the state) to kill.

It seems therefore obvious to me that the question of the sanctity of human life is a bedrock of Christian morals. If the protection of human life from conception to natural death isn't essential to Christian teaching, what is? Surely, here we ought to find a sharp dichotomy between the modern Church and the modern world. Right?

Wrong. The plain fact is, things don't break down that way. On one side of the cultural divide are not only secularists, but, alas, many liberal Protestants and some lapsed Catholics who, with trembling devotion to the spirit of the age, dutifully parrot the rhetoric that those who defend human life are "anti-choice."

On the other side of the divide are most Evangelicals, conservative members of the mainline Protestant churches, the Catholic and Orthodox churches, and conservative Jews. There's rich irony here. Not terribly long ago, these people (who tend to get tarred as "anti-choice fundamentalists") were attacked by secularists for *defending* Choice, not opposing it. That's because not terribly long ago, all the Advanced People were Marxists, materialists, and Skinnerian psychologists all agog for determinism and convinced that Choice (known then as Free Will) was sheer superstitious illusion.

These days, however, the fashion among Advanced People has changed, at least for the moment. Having finally discovered the reality of Choice, they have wrenched the cup of Free Will from the Church's grasp and drunk it to the dregs. Advanced People are now obsessed by Choice. Choice is the buzz-word of our time. Let us have Choice, no matter what we choose. Let all our choices be right and none wrong. In the name of Choice, let us destroy the weak one in order to save her. And let any who oppose this Truly Enlightened agenda be forever cast out as throwbacks to the Dark Ages.

Now the glorious fact is, there is a germ of truth in all this shrill railing against orthodox Christian belief. The champions of the unborn, the sick, and the aging *do* have allies in the Christian church, not only in the present but in the past. For not only the "Dark Ages" but absolutely *all* of Christianity for twenty centuries stands staunchly behind these defenseless ones against the extremely recent theologically liberal apologists for the culture of death. Indeed, so recent is the minting of this timeless "right" that not even theological liberals were willing to call abortion anything other than a grave sin until the past few decades. That is why we can scarcely find a shred of Christian theology written in favor of abortion and euthanasia before the 1960s and '70s. From the first century to the present, a shoreless ocean of testimony from every sector of the Church decries this terrible crime against God and humanity. And we Evangelicals, with very few exceptions, are of one voice with twenty centuries of Christian preaching concerning this most elementary of Christian moral truths.

I am proud to number myself among the ranks of pro-life Christians and will never waver from this commitment. But as I began to argue my position with liberal Christians who supported the so-called "right to choose," I did begin to waver in something: my conviction that the irrefutable basis for our pro-life conviction as Evangelicals is Scripture alone.

I know the verses that are quoted. "For you created my inmost being; you knit me together in my mother's womb" (Ps 139:13), "Before I formed you in the womb I knew you" (Jer 1:5) and so forth. I certainly agree that these verses bear oblique witness to a pro-life position. Indeed, I emphatically agree that the pro-life position is an obvious fact of Christian teaching throughout out all ages. But in arguing the matter with other Christians who read the same Bible I do, I began to realize that

I could not make opposition to abortion and devotion to the sanctity of preborn life an intrinsic, absolutely essential, utterly non-negotiable part of the Christian faith on the basis of Scripture alone. For the fact is, a modern apologist for the culture of death can and does argue that Scripture alone, apart from tradition, is as ambiguous about abortion as it is about the question of just war vs. pacifism — and therefore abortion is a matter of "Christian liberty."

Consider: neither testament gives a clear understanding of the status of unborn life. Is the fetus a human person possessing the same dignity as a child after birth? Is the conceptus? Is the act of directly causing the death of such a one an act of murder or some lesser offense? Is it an offense at all? No direct answer is ever attempted to these questions anywhere in Scripture.

Worse, the indirect ways in which Scripture addresses these issues are very oblique and open to multiple interpretations — apart from tradition. Thus Exodus 21:22 reads:

> If men who are fighting hit a pregnant woman and she gives birth prematurely but there is no serious injury, the offender must be fined whatever the woman's husband demands and the court allows. But if there is serious injury, you are to take life for life, eye for eye, tooth for tooth, hand for hand, foot for foot, burn for burn, wound for wound, bruise for bruise.

Far more questions are raised by this passage than are answered — if we are left to interpret it without reference to Jewish and Christian tradition as certain pro-choice Christians urge us to do. For instance, the Hebrew word which is here translated "gives birth prematurely" is, in fact, much more flexible than this. It means "departs" and can be read as "gives birth prematurely" or as "spontaneously aborts." So does the caveat about "serious injury" apply to the woman or to the miscarried child? Does the Law demand wound for wound for the mother's injury or the unborn's? If the mother is not seriously injured but the child dies, is this what is meant by "no serious injury"? The text does not say. Nor does the rest of Scripture help us.

Similarly, the New Testament does not tell us how to understand another difficult Old Testament passage: Numbers 5:20-27. This strange text prescribes an ordeal for suspected adulteresses, in which the suspected woman is placed under oath and made to drink "bitter water that brings a curse." The purpose of the ordeal was to call down a divine curse on the adulteress which, if she is guilty, will "enter into her and cause bitter pain, her womb shall discharge, [and] her uterus drop" (NRSV). What was discharged was the child conceived in adultery.

Thus, if we do not have any larger tradition for understanding such a text — if we "let Scripture interpret Scripture" as we Evangelicals say — it seems that Scripture does not automatically give one the impression that it lends itself to an irrefutable case for the sanctity of every human life from conception to natural death.

At this, we Evangelicals may attempt to create that larger interpretive context by "letting Scripture interpret Scripture" again. We might raise the counter-example of John the Baptist, moved by the Spirit in Elizabeth's womb when Mary arrived (Lk 1:41). Is not this a strong indication that even unborn children are persons responsive to the Spirit of God? Is it not a pretty darn good hint that unborn babies are people too?

Of course it is. That is, it's a "strong indication" — a hint, a sign, a good possibility. It is *not* incontrovertible *proof* that all children are similarly graced with supernatural gifts, including the supernatural gift of personhood, when they are as yet unformed in their mother's womb. Thus, I know Christians who have actually taken this text as license for first-trimester abortions since babies cannot be felt to kick *in utero* before the second trimester. Such Christians are living proof that the bare text of Scripture, apart from the interpretive tradition of Christendom, says nothing clear and definite about abortion or human development anywhere. Instead it gives *only* signs, clues, and hints which individual Christians, forsaking that tradition, can and do interpret in ways that directly contradict one another.

"OK," the Evangelical says. "Maybe John the Baptist isn't a biblical pro-life proof, but what about our Lord himself? Surely the personhood of the Second Person of the Trinity at his conception lends his dignity to all human beings from conception onwards so that 'whatever you did for one of the least of these' (Mt 25:40) applies supremely here."

Now I happen to agree with this argument. But I have spoken with other well-meaning, Bible-believing Christians (most of them strongly pro-life) who don't. They see no such extension of Christ's dignity to us by the mere fact that Christ was born a human being. They note that Christ is speaking of the "least of these brothers of *mine*" and argue that we become his brothers and God's children, not by being born but by being born again. They fear that to protect the unborn child on *this* basis is to ultimately mislead people into thinking we are holy when we are merely human.

Of course, I have counter-arguments to all this and they, of course, have counter-counter-arguments till between us you can't count the counters. But this is hardly evidence of the undeniable clarity of Scripture alone on this crucial point of Christian ethics.

"Well then," someone proposes, "maybe Scripture says so little because abortion was unheard of at the time? After all, you don't pass laws against speeding if no one has yet invented the automobile."

The difficulty with this theory is that it simply isn't true. Abortion predates Christianity by centuries and it flourished in pagan culture then as it flourishes in our quasi-pagan culture now. That is why the Didache, a manual of Christian instruction composed around 80 A.D., during the lifetime of the Apostle John and the gospel writers, commands: "You shall not procure an abortion. You shall not destroy a new-born child." Nor was the Didache alone in this. The subsequent writings of the post-apostolic period are simply unanimous when it comes to the Christian teaching on this subject. The epistle of Barnabas,[2] the letter to Diognetus,[3] the writings of Athenagoras,[4] Tertullian,[5] Hippolytus,[6] Origen,[7] Epiphanius,[8] Jerome, and a vast army of the Fathers, indeed every last Christian theologian who addresses this question until late in this century says exactly the same thing: abortion is a grave evil and the taking of human life.

Yet the odd thing is this: the old writers, the Fathers of the Church closest in time to the apostles, speak of their doctrine both in this area and in many others as definitely decided by the mind of the Church and the tradition of the apostles. For them, abortion is contrary, not so much to the Bible, as to the Holy Faith they received from their predecessors. Thus Basil the Great writes (c. 374): "A woman who has deliberately destroyed a fetus must pay the penalty for murder" and "Those also who give drugs causing abortions are murderers themselves, as well as those who receive the poison which kills the fetus."[9] Yet, for Basil, as for the rest of the Fathers, this teaching like many others has been preserved, not only in Scripture, but "in the Church."[10] As he himself says:

> Of the dogmas and kerygmas preserved in the Church, some we possess from written teaching and others we receive from the tradition of the Apostles, handed on to us in mystery. In respect to piety both are of the same force. No one will contradict any of these, no one, at any rate, who is even moderately versed in matters ecclesiastical. Indeed, were we to try to reject unwritten customs as having no great authority, we would unwittingly injure the Gospel in its vitals.[11]

In short, the Faith of which the Fathers speak (including its pro-life ethic) is revealed, not merely by Scripture alone, but by

Scripture rightly understood (and only *rightly understood) in the context of a larger tradition which is just as much from God as the Scripture it interprets.*

And no one, least of all we Evangelicals, questioned this pro-life teaching until this century. An unqualified reverence for human life from conception onward was universally a part of the essence of Christian belief and practice for all of Christian history until very recently. Indeed, the overwhelming number of Evangelicals quite faithfully followed this tradition without it even occurring to us to question it. Why was this, if we were truly deriving our beliefs from the clear and unambiguous teaching of the Bible alone, speaking forth only what Scripture spoke, keeping silent where Scripture was silent, and not binding the conscience of the believer on those questions in which Scripture permits different interpretations?

As with the Tradition of the Table of Contents, the obvious answer seemed to be that I was looking at another facet of extra-biblical *paradosis* which is so profoundly part of our bones that we Evangelicals never thought to distinguish it from (much less oppose it to) the Scriptures themselves. Indeed, as I looked at it, I began to realize that *the total pro-life* paradosis *was Scripture and tradition together*; distinct, yet an organic unity like the head and the heart, the right hand and the left. The Scripture gave light, but a very scattered light on this most crucial of issues. The *tradition* acted like a lens bringing that dancing light into focus. Tradition without Scripture was a darkened lens without a light; but likewise, Scripture without tradition was, on this vital issue, a blurry, unfocused light without a lens.

In realizing this, I realized Evangelicals were no different from Catholics on this score. Like all Christians before us till the time of the Didache, we were not treating this tradition — the Tradition of Pro-life Interpretation — as a fallible human reading of Scripture. Rather we treated it as absolutely authoritative and therefore as *revealed*.

Polygamy

The next test of the theory that we Evangelicals derive our essential beliefs from the Bible alone was sparked by something I remembered about two of the greatest figures of Protestant history.

In college I had run across the peculiar fact that John Milton, the great Puritan poet and author of *Paradise Lost*, thought that monogamy was unbiblical and had written against it (though he did not actually act on his principles). Milton seems have had pious reasons for his views: he wished to preserve the biblical patriarchs against what he saw as a threat against their holiness. Milton thought that if polygamy were forbidden, then he "should be forced to exclude from the sanctuary of God as spurious, the holy offspring which sprang from them, yea, the whole of the sons of Israel, for whom the sanctuary itself was made."[12] So he wrote, "Either therefore polygamy is a true marriage, or all children born in that state are spurious; which would include the whole race of Jacob, the twelve holy tribes chosen by God."[13]

Of course, Milton is remembered primarily as a poet, not a theologian, though he knew his Bible extremely well. Since his views on polygamy were thoroughly at odds with mainstream Christian thinking, I chalked up my discovery as a historical curiosity of the English Reformation. But to my surprise, years later I discovered that another Bible-believing figure in Protestant history held similar views, and he is not so easily dismissed. His name was Martin Luther.

Luther, it seems, was confronted with the question of whether or not the Landgrave Philip of Hesse, an important official of his day, might enter into a bigamous marriage. When pressed to render a judgment in the matter, Luther (together with Philip Melancthon) concluded that monogamy was no necessary part of the Christian revelation and that polygamy was a legitimate practice for a Christian.[14] In his words:

> I confess that I cannot forbid a person to marry

> several wives, for it does not contradict the
> Scripture. If a man wishes to marry more than
> one wife he should be asked whether he is sat-
> isfied in his conscience that he may do so in
> accordance with the word of God. In such a
> case the civil authority has nothing to do in
> such a matter.[15]

Like Milton, Luther found that the universal Christian condemnation of polygamy was not really provable from Scripture alone. For him, it was therefore a matter of Christian
liberty.

Now it may be objected that polygamy is hardly the live
issue abortion is today. After all, who but a few guests on tab-
loid TV have advocated a return to it in our society? Indeed,
Luther and Milton are extraordinary exceptions to the otherwise universal Christian condemnation of polygamy — a condemnation heartily shared by Dr. James Dobson, Chuck
Swindoll, John MacArthur, and all other committed, Bible-only
Evangelicals.

And yet . . . where does this condemnation come from? For
as Milton and Luther pointed out, it is *scarcely supported by
Scripture*.

"Nonsense," said my Evangelical friends. "Jesus forbade
polygamy by his words, 'Anyone who divorces his wife and
marries another woman commits adultery against her. And if
she divorces her husband and marries another man, she commits adultery' " (Mk 10:11-12).

Yet this only proves my point. For such an understanding of
our Lord's words depends entirely on the *way* in which the
Church habitually reads these words, not on the bare text alone.
That is, it depends on a Tradition of Monogamy and not merely
on the text. For if we read the text strictly, as Milton and Luther
did, we find it only speaks of *divorce* and remarriage. It nowhere forbids men multiple wives if they retain previous ones.
So, in this area also, we Evangelicals derive our belief from

Scripture *as it has always been understood by the mind of the Church, both Protestant and Catholic.*

Now it may be objected that I am adding a needless interpreter. After all, Paul makes abundantly clear that remarriage (not to mention multiple marriage) is forbidden while one's spouse is still living (Rom 7:3; 1 Cor 7:39). And this is true enough — for women. But what of *men* hailing from either a first-century pagan or Jewish culture, both of which permitted male polygamy?

If we follow the great Evangelical maxim and "let Scripture interpret Scripture," we are given biblical figures such as Jacob, David, and Solomon, all of whom are spoken of with great approval by God himself and none of whom are informed that male polygamy per se is a sin.

If we counter by saying "Jacob's two wives were a nuisance to him (and he to them)," I reply, Jacob's many sons were a nuisance too, but Scripture still says "be fruitful and multiply." If we retort, "Solomon's many pagan wives turned his heart after other gods," I reply that the problem, according to Scripture, was that they were pagan, not that they were many (1 Kgs 11:2-6). If we cite the command in Deuteronomy 17:17 warning against having many wives, we must also note that the same passage (v. 16) warns against having many horses. Does the Law therefore forbid a man to have more than one horse as well? Letting Scripture interpret Scripture, it would appear this is not the intent of the Deuteronomic warning since David is specifically told by God that *his* many wives were given into his arms by the Lord himself and were, apparently, part of the many blessings God heaped on him (2 Sm 12:8). Rather, the passage in Deuteronomy is quite clearly a warning against greed, not against polygamy.

Now let us be clear. I am not Joseph Smith or Hugh Hefner. I do not advocate a return to male polygamy or the keeping of harems. Rather, my point is that Christianity has *never* advocated polygamy — has opposed it always and everywhere as a thing essentially contrary to the will of God *despite* what the

Old Testament appears to say. And we Evangelicals stand un-
reservedly on this fact and regard male polygamy not merely as
chauvinistic and impractical, but as obvious sin.

Yet, we have little cause to do so on the basis of Scripture
alone, as Luther and Milton cogently argue.

To be sure, letting Scripture interpret Scripture would not
make taking another person's wife or husband any less a sin.
That remains strictly forbidden in both Old and New Testament
documents (Prov 7:6-27; Mk 10: 11-12). So is abandoning the
wife of one's youth (Mal 2:15). So is marrying outside the Faith
(Ez 9:1-2; 1 Cor 7:39; 2 Cor 6:14). So is polygamy by a woman
(1 Cor 7:39). So too is the sin of divorcing one's wife (and
thereby leaving her, in first-century culture, with but one choice
in order to avoid starvation or prostitution: remarriage and therefore adultery) (Mt. 5:32). But, with one minor exception, *nowhere* is a man forbidden to take more than one wife at a time.

That exception is Paul's command to overseers (and *only*
overseers) to be a husband of "but one wife" (1 Tm 3:2; Ti 1:6).
Yet the very fact that Paul gives this command only to overseers (bishops) suggests (if we have no tradition outside Scripture) that other Christian men could have more than one if they
liked. After all, if monogamy were as crucial as we believe it to
be and if Paul were preaching in a culture which still embraced
polygamy, one would expect it to be a fairly constant theme in
his moral teaching. Yet in all his other discussions of "practical
Christian living" in every book from Romans to Philemon, Paul
never mentions a demand for monogamy on the part of the rank-
and-file believer, even in strongly polygamous pagan cultures
like Corinth. On the contrary, only in his instructions to overseers, whose special responsibilities demand simplicity of life,
does Paul mention this demand for monogamy. Small wonder
Milton and Luther, relying on Scripture alone, came to view it
as optional.

And yet we Evangelicals (and Lutherans and Puritans) ignore these champions of purely biblical revelation and treat
monogamy, not as a matter of liberty very weakly attested by

Scripture, but as a self-evident aspect of the Faith incumbent on every Christian. Further, we do so, not on the basis of polygamy's impracticality or incongeniality to feminism, but on the firm conviction that *God* calls it a sin as well. And the Church for its entire history holds this view, even when polygamy was perfectly acceptable to the larger culture, both Jewish and pagan.

Which brought me to a puzzle.

One the one hand, I could see how American Christians at the end of the twentieth century could certainly be culturally conditioned to regard polygamy as dead. Commonsense, peer pressure, and feminism would be a strong deterrent to any lingering vestiges of Old World chauvinism left in the American male psyche.

But how does this modern culture shift account for the fact that polygamy was just as dead in fourth-century Christian teaching, when feminism was not a particularly commanding presence in the media and ordinary culture was enthusiastic about male polygamy? Basil the Great had never seen a copy of *Ms Magazine* and was surrounded by a fourth-century culture uninfluenced by the monogamous writings of Focus on the Family. Nonetheless Basil wrote of multiple marriage that "such a state is no longer called marriage but polygamy or, indeed, a moderate fornication."[16] Those engaged in it were ordered by him to be excommunicated for up to five years and to be restored to fellowship "only after they have shown some fruitful repentance."[17] This opposition to polygamy, Basil makes clear, is not something he invented any more than Dr. Dobson did. On the contrary, Basil says that these teachings are "accepted as our usual practice, not from the canons but in conformity with our predecessors."[18] In other words, not from the apostolic writings but from the *tradition* in force in the whole Church from its remotest antiquity.

But surely, I thought, this is very odd. I had been taught that the embrace of extra-biblical tradition always represented a move *toward* paganism, not away from it. It was my understanding that the early Church had departed from the high and hard truth of the Bible after the death of the apostles and, seeking human approval, had allowed all sorts of pagan notions to creep in (like purgatory, devotion to Mary, superstitions about relics, and so forth). Why then, with all this "pagan creep" going on, would the Church staunchly oppose both paganism and Judaism in the matter of polygamy when the Bible was very ambiguous on the matter? Surely if one was going to accommodate paganism it would be here, wouldn't it?

Yet the facts were clear: even though male polygamy was lawful in both pagan culture and in the Old Testament, even though polygamy continues to this day among Jews in Muslim countries,[19] even though Jesus and the apostles never speak against it in the Scriptures explicitly as a moral norm for all believers, still the post-apostolic Church, claiming apostolic tradition as its authority, speaks against it as plainly contrary to the teaching of Christ and does everything it can to root out the practice as quickly as possible. Indeed, the early Church's depth of conviction is so strong that it reverberates throughout the Protestant world for four centuries after the break with Catholicism. Moreover, it remains so strong down to the present that it almost never occurred to us Evangelicals (or anyone else) to question whether there is any other way of reading our Bibles. Everybody (even an unbeliever) knows that the ban on polygamy is an essential, non-negotiable part of Christian teaching and always has been.

And yet, I asked myself, if this is not treating tradition like revelation, what is it?

The Trinity

To all of the above, a convinced multiculturalist Christian might have a rejoinder, however. He might, for instance, say to some missionary in Muslim lands, "Who are you to impose your values and ask the Muslim to renounce his customary acceptance of polygamy? Bring him the gospel, to be sure. But don't force your Western interpretation of Scripture on him and cause him to stumble." Similarly, there are brother and sister Protestants of the liberal variety who are willing to say, "Abortion is *not* necessarily a sin by biblical lights. We will simply have to treat it as a matter of Christian liberty, like we did with artificial contraception earlier in this century. But on the really *biblical* essentials of Christianity, I'm solid. That is why I don't go in for either Catholic traditions or for right-wing Evangelical ones lifted from Catholicism. I'm just a straightforward trinitarian Christian without a right-wing political ax to grind."

To this I raise two objections.

First, playing this sort of "Simon says" game with Scripture, looking only for direct and explicit proof texts and flatly ignoring unanimous tradition where it also speaks as revelation for twenty centuries, leads to a lot more than loose attitudes toward sex. Abortion and polygamy are not the only issues ambiguously addressed by Scripture. A "Simon says" hermeneutic also transforms necrophilia, tissue harvesting of anesthetized condemned prisoners, genetic experimentation, slaughter of civilian populations in war, and many other outrages into matters of personal taste, cultural whim, or political expedience. When this happens, the Christian's own "Simon says" theology prevents him from working against the power of the state or the culture to prevent these evils.

However, even this is small beer from an eternal perspective. The question "How shall we then live?" is less grave than the ultimate problem posed by Christ himself: "Who do you say I am?" Even if we assume the validity of the canon of Scripture, a strictly Bible-only form of revelation *still* cannot get us to our orthodox Evangelical answer to Christ's question. Indeed we cannot remain Evangelical in any meaningful sense at all without treating tradition as though it also preserves revelation. For as I discovered, "straightforward" trinitarianism, which is an absolutely essential hallmark of Evangelicalism, is just as dependent on tradition's reading of Scripture as the ethical strictures we have examined.

What could be more central to Evangelical belief than the

deity of Christ? This was the very issue that had spurred me to battle with modernism. It is the great thundering truth proclaimed by every good preacher of the gospel. If that is not essential Christianity, then there is no such thing as Christianity. Yet as I began to read Scripture and look at church history, I began to realize there are more ways in heaven and earth of attacking the deity of Christ than modernism has dreamed of in its philosophy. There are ways that need never pursue any such crudities as declaring our Lord the product of a rape or asserting that he was eaten by wild dogs. Indeed, there are ways of denying the deity of Christ which can easily slip in under the Evangelical radar screen, ways which reverence him as a supernatural being and call loudly for trust in Scripture as the one and only source of revelation, yet which firmly consign Christ to the status of mere creature just as surely as the most ardent skeptic.

Most famous among these ways is a third-century movement known as Arianism.

Arians were principally concerned to preserve the Oneness of God from pagan polytheism. They argued cogently from Scripture. They were well-trained, Greek-speaking theologians who could read Scripture in the original tongues. The only problem was that they had the brighter, simpler idea that Jesus was not truly God but only a sort of godlet or superior created being.

In defense of this idea, the Arians rejected tradition and pointed to texts like "the Father is greater than I" (Jn 14:28) and "Why do you call me good? . . . No one is good — except God alone" (Mk 10:18). They also pointed to the form of the Trinity as found in Paul: "God, Jesus Christ, the Holy Spirit."[20] They could come up with plausible explanations for terms and expressions which we Evangelicals thought could only point to Christ's divinity. For example, Arians said the statement, "I and the Father are one" (Jn 10:30) refers to oneness of *purpose*, not oneness of being. They pointed out that Scripture refers to supernatural created beings as "sons of God" (Job 38:7 NAB) without intending they are one in being with the Father. They observed that even mere humans were called "gods" (Ps 82:6; Jn 10:34-36), without the implication that they are God. Therefore they inferred that the Son, supernatural though he may be (as angels, principalities, and powers are supernatural), is neither co-eternal with the Father nor one in being with him.

Now many Christians today regard all this wrangling over technical philosophical phrases like "co-eternal" and "of one being" as just so much theological technobabble. We lament that the early Church got so hung up on "cold Christs and tangled Trinities." We shake our heads and say we need to forget all that head knowledge and just magnify the Lord Jesus and worship him. We say well-intended things like, "Let's just get back to basics and return to the simple biblical message that Christ died for us to take away our sins and give us a share in the life of God by the Holy Spirit."

But this simple biblical message is precisely what Arianism denies — and it uses the Bible to do it! To deny that Christ is one in being with the Father is to deny that he can ever be magnified and worshiped because it is to deny that he is God. To deny that he is God is to deny that his death meant any more for a sinful humanity than the death of any other creature. Likewise it is to deny that he can ever give us a share in the life of God. Even the Son, however glorious, cannot give what he does not have.

How would we Evangelicals argue against Arianism using Scripture alone? We'd say that John speaks of the "only begotten " and says of him that he "was God" and was "with God in the beginning" (Jn 1:1-2, 18; 3:16 KJV). We would reply that, although the *term* "Trinity" is not in Scripture, nonetheless the *concept* of Trinity is there.

But a good Arian would be quick to point out that God plainly says "You are my Son; today I have become your Father" (Heb 1:5) which implies that there was a time *before* the Son was begotten. Thus, though the Son was with God in the beginning of his creative work, says the Arian, that doesn't mean he wasn't created himself.

In other words, the Arian can argue that there was a time

when the Son was not. But there was never a time when the Father was not. He is without beginning. Therefore, according to the Arian, the Son is *not* God in the same sense as the Father and does not share his eternal, beginningless essence. This amounts to a denial of the deity of Christ since a God with a beginning is not the God of Israel. Great and glorious and supernatural as he may be compared to the rest of creation (and Paul implies he is a creature when he calls him the firstborn over all *creation* [Col 1:15] doesn't he?), nonetheless he is *only* a creature, says the Arian.

But that would not be the end of it. For the Arian would likewise preserve the oneness of God by insisting that the Holy Spirit is not a person, much less the Third Person of the Trinity. Can an Evangelical appealing to Scripture alone definitively disprove *this* claim?

Maybe. But then . . . maybe not.

To be sure, the Spirit is spoken of as a Paraclete (a defense lawyer [Jn 14:16]) and is referred to as engaging in personal acts such as convicting of sin (Jn 16:8), bearing witness (Jn 15:26), giving joy (Lk 10:21), enabling saints to perform miracles and prophecy (1 Cor 12), and so on. Similarly, we Evangelicals would argue that he can be blasphemed, grieved, insulted, and lied to (Mk 3:29; Eph 4:30; Acts 5:3).

But on the other hand, says the Arian, the New Testament word for "Spirit" is neuter and the Greek often refers to the Spirit as "it." Likewise, it speaks of the Spirit in non-personal images as well. The Spirit is a fire (Acts 2:3), a dove (Mt 3:16), a rushing wind (Acts 2:2), a fountain of water (Jn 7:37-39). The Spirit "fills" people like an impersonal wine poured into a bottle (Acts 2:4). Come to think of it, says the Arian, Scripture *often* speaks of abstract things in personal terms. Thus it portrays sin "crouching at your door" like a bandit (Gen 4:7), earth crying out at the blood of Abel (Gen 4:10), wisdom as a woman working at God's side (Prov 8), and the law of sin waging war against the law of Paul's mind like a soldier (Rom 7:23). So, says the Arian, the Scriptures which appear to portray the Spirit as a person are in fact personalized images of the power of God, not a revelation of a Third Person in the Godhead.

Evangelicals may well counter that Paul specifically declares that the Lord is the Spirit (2 Cor 3:18). But the Arian has a ready answer. Granted, he says, the Spirit is spoken of as "the Lord" now and then. But there are also many passages in which creatures speak and are addressed as though they are God himself (Gen 18). So Paul's language need not necessarily mean that the Spirit is literally God Almighty.

Very well then, is my point, "Be Arian"? No. My point is that an Evangelical, relying on Scripture alone and "never binding the conscience of the believer on those questions in which Scripture permits different interpretations," is in a poor position to say definitively, "*Don't* be Arian." Arianism has just the sort of scriptural ammo which today leads, not so much to a triumph of Arianism as to a stalemate between Arianism and orthodoxy in the Evangelical arena.

For Arian "simplicity" is not dead. Indeed, that enormous marketplace of ideas called the Internet teems with Arians from various sects who have a field day as simply an "alternative Christian theology" and we Bible-only Evangelicals are remarkably weak in argument with them. (The summary of Arian/orthodox debate given above is culled from long experience of watching such arguments on the Internet.) I cannot count the times I have seen orthodox Evangelicals finally retreat from the issue with a fuddled shrug and some muttered variation on, "Well, I just feel you're wrong." Yet this is tantamount to telling the confused non-Christian that Christianity is 1) whatever we fell like, or 2) an irrational belief in the impossible.

How then, I wondered, can we even be sure of *this* foundation stone of the Faith (much less communicate it to others) if the ambiguity of Scripture made it too a "matter of liberty" according to our own Evangelical criteria?

I discovered the answer as I listened to one of those radio call-in shows where theologians tackle various questions about the Bible. The host of this show was a solid Evangelical with a high regard for the Bible who was always very careful to speak of Scripture alone as the bottom line of revelation. Yet the odd thing was, when a particularly articulate exponent of anti-trinitarianism called and pointed out the typical Arian readings of various Scriptures, the host had one final bottom line *below* the bottom line. After citing various counter-Scriptures (and receiving more plausible Arian readings by the caller until yet another stalemate seemed imminent), the host finally said, in essence, "Your interpretation is simply not what historic Christianity has ever understood its own Bible to mean." He then asked the Arian caller if he was really prepared to insist that twenty centuries of Christians (including people who had heard the apostles with their own ears and who clearly regarded Jesus as God) had been utterly wrong about the central fact of their faith while he alone was right.

This made sense. It seemed plain to me that it was idle for the Arian caller to wrench Scripture away from twenty centuries of ordinary Christian interpretation of so crucial a matter and declare the entire Church, from those who knew the apostles down to the present, incapable of understanding what it meant in its own Scriptures concerning so fundamental an issue. To deny that the deity of Christ was part of the apostolic preaching is to say that the apostles managed to leave a wildly blasphemous impression upon their fledgling churches when really they had no such intention. It is to assert that everywhere — north, south, east, and west, among Jews and Gentiles, across a bewildering smorgasbord of ethnicities, cultures, languages, and peoples from Palestine to Asia to Greece to Rome to Spain to Africa to India to Gaul — the apostles managed to fix in the minds of every one of their churches something they had not meant: that the mere creature called Jesus is "our God,"[21] "the True God existing before the ages"[22] who was "born in the form of a man."[23] Quite a little mixup indeed! If only the Twelve hadn't mumbled so, their disciples would not have gotten so confused about such an elementary thing as the distinction between Creator and creature!

Is it even remotely likely that the entire early Church mis-understood the apostles that badly? Is it not obvious that the churches preserved the plain apostolic meaning of the Scriptures by carrying in their bosom not only the text of Scripture, but the clear memory of the *way* in these texts were intended by the apostles? Was it not obvious that this living memory was, in fact, essential to correctly reading the Scripture and that without it, the Arian was taking the Bible itself out of context?

But in seeing this, I couldn't help seeing something else: my Evangelical radio show host (like my Evangelical friends and me) was saying that a Tradition of Trinitarian Interpretation living in the Church was just as essential and revealed as the Scripture being interpreted. When we spoke of the absolute union of the Father and the Son, of the Holy Spirit as God Almighty and the Creator of all things, we Evangelicals were in fact resting serenely, not on the Bible alone, but on the Bible in union with the interpretative tradition of the Church just as we rested serenely on its Tradition of the Table of Contents, its Tradition of the Sanctity of Human Life, and its Tradition of Monogamy.

This again meant that whatever we Evangelicals *said* about tradition being "useful but not essential" to Christian revelation, we *behaved* exactly as though we believed trinitarian tradition — a tradition both in union with and yet distinct from the Scripture it interprets — is the other leg upon which the revelation of Christ's deity and the Spirit's Lordship stands. Once again we were treating Scripture and tradition, neither as competitors nor as identical, but as light and lens.

Yeah, But . . .

None of my toying with tradition-as-revelation sat well with my Evangelical friends. They were naturally nervous about just where my thoughts were taking me. They felt, as I had once felt, that such talk could only lead to embracing the traditions of men and adding them to the word of God. They said that to talk of extra-biblical revelation was to talk like a Mormon. How, they asked, was I supposed to avoid gluing a bunch of new stuff on to my Christian faith like a latter-day Joseph Smith once I accepted the principle of extra-biblical revelation? Wasn't this what I had set out to oppose in modernism? If I wanted extra-biblical revelation, why not just start adding some more books to the Bible right now? But if I wasn't willing to do that (and I wasn't), then why not acknowledge what all true Christians acknowledged: that public revelation was complete and closed with the death of the apostles?

This jarred me. But not for the reasons my friends supposed. Because where they saw a clincher of an argument against tradition as revelation, I was beginning at last to see how the Catholic Church might be on to something with all this extra-biblical tradition stuff.

For my friends were perfectly right. It *is* a belief absolutely essential to all orthodox Christians that, as the Second Vatican Council says, "no new public revelation is to be expected before the glorious manifestation of our Lord Jesus Christ."[24] But this immediately raised two questions:

First, why did the Catholic Church regard this teaching as dogma when Mormonism explicitly denied it? If Rome's assertion that Sacred Tradition is revelatory was identical to the Mormon claim of continuing revelation, why then did Rome diametrically oppose Salt Lake City by insisting public revelation could not be added to?

Secondly, where did we Evangelicals and Rome *get* this rock-bottom, non-negotiable belief that public revelation was closed? As I reflected on it, I realized this belief is simply *nowhere* to be found in any explicit Scripture. There is not one single syllable anywhere in the New Testament which says that public revelation will close when the apostles shuffle off their mortal coil.[25] To be sure, such a view of revelation can, given the right interpretive lens of Tradition, be seen to be implied by certain extremely oblique texts in the letters to Timothy and Titus. But practically all the work is being done by the lens, since there is extraordinarily little scriptural light to focus.

Therefore, if we hold (as my friends and I did) that this teaching is rock bottom apostolic revelation honored by all true Christians, we are, paradoxically enough, saying that the only way this could have come to us from the apostles was via extrabiblical tradition. Thus, the Tradition of the Closure of Public Revelation is yet another facet of the unwritten *paradosis* which everybody — Catholic and Protestant — treats as equal in weight to the truth contained in Scripture. Everyone regards this tradition as absolutely crucial for framing the *way* in which we do and do not read Scripture. So once again, our actual practice as Evangelicals seemed to be better accounted for by Catholic theology than by our own.

It was then a plain mistake to think we Evangelicals spoke forth only what Scripture spoke, kept silent where Scripture was silent, and never bound the conscience of the believer on those questions in which Scripture permits different interpretations. On the contrary, we lived (and had to live) by tradition almost as deeply as any Catholic. For us, as for Rome, tradition was the lens that focused the light of Scripture. For us, as for Rome, that tradition was not a pair of "useful but not necessary" disposable glasses; it was the lens of our living eye and the heart of vision. It was so much a part of us that we were oblivious to it. I realized we Evangelicals had been so focused on the light of Scripture that we had forgotten the lens through which we looked.

But now I was aware of the lens of tradition. I was aware that it is both in union with and distinct from Scripture. I was aware that apart from it essential elements of Christian faith and ethics remain permanently in the twilight zone. I was aware that such tradition is of great antiquity and strongly points back to the apostles themselves. And I was aware that this lens of tradition was in every eye, both Protestant and Catholic.

So, being aware of all this, I returned to the question which had so perplexed me when the problem of the canon had first presented itself. "Why," I had demanded, "is the canon of Scripture not a human tradition?"

In reply, Scripture had shown me a continuous thread of

reliance on extra-biblical tradition on the part of both Old and New Testament figures led by Jesus Christ himself. It had shown me plainly worded instructions from Paul demanding that I hold to tradition whether it was written or unwritten. The writings of the seminal figures in the early Church following the apostles revealed a Church which had followed this command. They frankly declared of their doctrine that (in Basil the Great's words) "some we possess from written teaching and others we receive from the tradition of the Apostles."

Finally, to crown it all, I had discovered that Evangelicals were, in fact, participating in this tradition in at least five crucial areas of our ethics and theology without our even realizing it. And as I saw all this, I found for the first time that a new question was beginning to form in my mind:

What if the canon of Scripture is part of the Tradition, not of men, but of God?

Notes

1. *Miracles* (New York: Macmillan, 1947), p. 40.
2. *Epistle of Barnabas*, 19, 5.
3. *Letter to Diognetus*, 5, 6.
4. Athenagoras, *Prebia peri Christianon*, 35.
5. Tertullian, *Apology*, 9.
6. Hippolytus, *Refutation of All Heresies*, 9, 12.
7. Origen, *Contra Haereses*, 9.
8. Epiphanius, *Panarion*, PG 41, 339.
9. Letter of Basil the Great to Ampliochius, Bishop of Iconium: *The First Canonical Letter*, 188:2; 188, 8.
10. Basil the Great, *The Holy Spirit*, 27, 66.
11. Ibid.
12. John Milton, "The Christian Doctrine," Chapter 10 in *John Milton: Complete Poems and Major Prose*, Merrit Y. Hughes, ed. (New York: The Odyssey Press, 1957), p. 994.
13. Ibid.

14. Owen Chadwick, *The Reformation* (London: Penguin Books, 1972), pp. 71-72.

15. Martin Luther, *De Wette*, II, 459.

16. Letter of Basil the Great to Ampliochius, Bishop of Iconium: *The First Canonical Letter*, 188, 4.

17. Ibid.

18. Ibid.

19. *New Bible Dictionary*, 2nd Edition, J.D. Douglas, Organizing Editor (Wheaton: Tyndale House, 1984), p. 743.

20. 2 Corinthians 13:13, for example, appears to distinguish, not the First Person of the Trinity from the other two Persons, but just plain "God" from Jesus Christ and the Holy Spirit, as though the latter two are in some sense subordinate creatures, not co-eternal members of the Godhead.

21. Ignatius, *Letter to the Romans*, 1, 1 (c. 110).

22. Melito of Sardes, *Fragment in Anastasius of Sinai*, 13, 73 (mid-second century).

23. Tatian, *Address to the Greeks*, 21 (second century).

24. Second Vatican Council, *Dogmatic Constitution on Divine Revelation*, 4.

25. That includes Revelation 22:18-19, which is a warning against adding and subtracting from the book of Revelation alone and has nothing whatever to do with promulgating a general doctrine that public revelation was complete with the end of the apostolic age.

CHAPTER SEVEN
THE TRADITION
OF GOD

How firm a foundation, ye saints of the Lord,
is laid for your faith in his excellent word! — John Rippon

I sat for some time drumming my fingers on my Bible in
thought and prayer. Up till now such claims on behalf of
tradition had always seemed bogus: a lot of Catholic theological fast talk for justifying unbiblical teachings. For years, I
had envisioned the guys at Trent and Vatican II saying, "Okay,
so purgatory *isn't* in Scripture! So what? It's in . . . uh . . . Tradition! Yeah! That's the ticket! *Tradition*!" Indeed, I had made
little distinction between such Catholic Tradition and the modernist attempts at subverting Scripture.

But now, what with the threat of modernism's deconstruction
of Scripture looming behind me and manifold evidence of a real
live extra-biblical *paradosis* popping up not only in Scripture
and Catholic theology but even in the everyday practice of my
native Evangelicalism, it was dawning on me that I had perhaps
been overhasty in equating the Catholic claim of Tradition-as-
revelation with modernist attempts to subvert the Bible. As I
prayed, I recalled again Paul's admonition to "Test *everything*.
Hold on to the good" (1 Thes 5:21) and asked nervously, "Even
Catholic teaching, Lord?" The question seemed to answer itself.

So I began perusing the *Catholic Catechism* by Father John Hardon, S.J., to see what I could see. As I did, I began to notice a remarkable difference between Sacred Tradition-believing Catholics and modernists who believed in . . . well, what *did* they believe in? Certainly they did not believe, as the Catholic Church did, that "Sacred Scripture is the word of God inasmuch as it is consigned to writing under the inspiration of the Holy Spirit."[1] They did not teach, as the Catholic Church did, that "in Sacred Scripture, God speaks through men in human fashion."[2] They emphatically did not hold, as the Catholic Church did, that "We must acknowledge that the books of Scripture, firmly, faithfully and without error, teach that truth which God, for the sake of our salvation, wished to see confided to the sacred Scriptures."[3] By some strange irony, the Catholic attitude toward Scripture, compared to modernism, sounded downright . . . *Evangelical!*

But Evangelical with this difference: the Catholic Church had never labored under the illusion of a self-attesting Scripture. Rather, it had avoided my many blind alleys by an ancient awareness that a Tradition of God *had* preserved revelation outside of Scripture and that "by means of the same Tradition the full canon of sacred books is known to the Church."[4]

Or as the *Catechism* elsewhere put it:

> Jesus Christ ordered his apostles, who are the source of all saving truth and moral teaching, to preach it to every creature. . . . [T]his truth and teaching are contained in written books *and* in the unwritten traditions that the apostles received from Christ himself or that were handed on, as it were from hand to hand, from the apostles under the inspiration of the Holy Spirit, and so have come down to us[5] [italics added].

I sat blinking at these words in excitement and not a little anxiety. They echoed precisely what I thought I had just discovered, but they were written by the Council of Trent in the mid-1500s! According to the Catholic Church, Tradition was not the human whim of a bunch of bishops, as the modernists held. Nor was Tradition swallowed by Scripture as my friends said. Nor was it a "useful but not essential" second banana to the Bible as the *New Bible Dictionary* said. On the contrary, the Catholic Church was adamant that:

> [I]t is not from Sacred Scripture alone that the Church draws her certainty about everything which has been revealed. *Both Sacred Tradition and Sacred Scripture are to be accepted and venerated with the same sense of loyalty and reverence*[6] [italics added].

According to the Catholic Church, both Scripture and Tradition were from Christ and made by him to stand inseparably united. The two were one — but not the same. They were the hydrogen and oxygen that fused to form living water. They were the words and the tune of a single song. They were two sides of the same apostolic coin. In short, by Catholic lights, the one apostolic *paradosis* of Christ was handed on in just the way Paul had said it should be: both by word of mouth and by letter.

But this raised a fresh problem. Didn't such thinking place the Church, a mere human community, before the inspired word of God? Was not the Church founded on the word of God, and not the word of God on the Church? Did not the Catholic view of revelation therefore set human wisdom above God's just as surely as modernism did?

It had long seemed so to me. For in a fuzzy way I had conceived of the Church as resting on Scripture the way the United States of America rested on the Constitution. I had vaguely believed the latter created and established the former. Yet in my asking the question, something clicked in my brain. It struck me that it was, as modernism had pointed out, strict historical accuracy to place the Church before the completed Bible — decades before it was all written and centuries before it was fully collated and canonized. That was why there was a Thessalonian Church for Paul to write the earliest parts of the New Testament to.

So the question grew in me: "If the early Church was not founded on the written Scriptures, in what sense *was* it 'founded on the word of God'?" To find out, I returned to the New Testament, and began by looking at the way in which its most famous convert, Paul, came by the gospel. What I found surprised me.

The conversion of Saul of Tarsus begins, not on the Damascus Road, but with the martyrdom of Stephen. Saul heard Stephen preach, and his preaching set goads in Saul's spirit (Acts 26:14). Yet the thing that distinguishes (and dooms) Stephen when he preaches to the Sanhedrin in Acts 7 is not his faith in Scripture, but his faith in the oral tradition of the apostles. After all, the elders and Saul know their Bible as well as Stephen. Both he and they have been reading it for years and are intimately familiar with its stories, lessons, and prophecies. But only Stephen sees his Bible focused through the lens of apostolic *paradosis*. It is this *paradosis* which provokes the elders (and also Saul) to notice something of a difference between the way they read their Bibles and the way Stephen reads his.

The interesting thing is that this difference in interpretation is not healed for Saul by more diligent Bible study or by "letting Scripture interpret Scripture" (as my Evangelical background urged). On the contrary, healing comes when Saul sees Scripture through the same lens by which Stephen saw it — a lens given by the revelation of Christ (on the Damascus Road) *and* by the *paradosis* of the apostles. For as Paul repeatedly affirms later, Christ not only revealed himself in that moment of mystical ecstasy; he just as reliably revealed himself through "what I received" from the apostles.

This came as a surprise to my friends. After all, didn't Paul say to the Galatians that he did not receive his gospel "from any man, nor was I taught it; rather, I received it by revelation from

Jesus Christ" (Gal 1:12). Yes. But he did not say this to issue a sweeping denial of any dependence on the teaching of the Twelve. Rather, he said it to deny the claims of certain people that he wasn't really an apostle and didn't really have authority from Christ.

To prove this, we need only note that Paul, a few lines later, notes that he made certain to have his preaching vetted by the Twelve, "for fear I was running or had run my race in vain" (Gal 2:2). Further, even a cursory reading of the New Testament shows that Paul has no difficulty relying on tons of apostolic Tradition in the form of doxologies (Gal 1:5; Phil 4:20; Rom 11:36; Eph 3:21), hymns (Phil 2:6-11; Col 1:15-20; Eph 5:14), stories (1 Cor 11:23-25), and prayers (1 Cor 16:22), which he faithfully passes along without blinking an eye. This is why, even though he did not know Christ during his earthly ministry, Paul can nonetheless frequently quote and allude to historical sayings of Christ (Acts 20:35), facts about his life, trial, death, resurrection, and ascension.[7] All these data are quite obviously treated by Paul as part of a common deposit of apostolic Tradition to which all Christians are privy, not as things mystically revealed to him on the Damascus Road.

So the mere fact that Christ once revealed himself to Paul without any human mediation does not mean Paul was not subsequently instructed in the faith of the Twelve by the Christian community. On the contrary, Paul deliberately "went up to Jerusalem to get acquainted with Peter and stayed with him fifteen days" (Gal 1:18). There he also met James. He spent years cooling his heels in Tarsus and Antioch before he was sent on his first mission. During that time he would have done what Scripture said all new Christians did: learning, as Hebrews puts it, the "elementary teachings about Christ" and "instruction about baptisms, the laying on of hands, the resurrection of the dead, and eternal judgement" (Heb 6:1-2). We forget that Paul was taught, like every other new Christian, that Christ had told the Twelve, "He who listens to you listens to me" (Lk 10:16), and thus to make no distinction whatever between the

Tradition of the apostles and the authoritative revelation of Christ. Forgetting this, we thus forget that Paul often appeals to this Tradition handed down from the Twelve — and that he does so in a way which plainly shows such Tradition is, for him, "from the Lord."

That is why Paul twice tells the Corinthians that "what I received I passed on to you" (1 Cor 11:23; 15:3). What did he receive? In this case, the teaching concerning the events surrounding the Lord's Supper and the Resurrection. From whom did he receive it? "From the Lord," says Paul. Is Paul therefore saying he was given direct, Spirit-infused knowledge of these events?

No. He is saying he was given an apostolic *paradosis*. For in using the terms "received and handed on," Paul is repeating standard rabbinical jargon which means literally, "I am transmitting, without addition or subtraction, a tradition I have been taught."[8] Since "he who listens to the apostles listens to Christ," Paul simply refers to the traditions as "from the Lord" since they are, in fact, the core of what the apostles have, by Christ's authority, drummed into their churches wherever they have gone.

That is why the two gospel stories he relates in 1 Corinthians (of the institution of the Lord's Supper and of the Resurrection) bear such a strong resemblance to other accounts of these events (in the written gospels) which are separated from this epistle by many years and many miles. Matthew, Mark, Luke, and Paul are drawing on a common *paradosis*, known to all the churches, which has set the words of the story in a sort of liturgical concrete that admits very little variation. It is precisely adherence to this common *paradosis* which Paul commends when he tells the Corinthians:

> I commend you because your remember me in
> everything and maintain the traditions even as
> I have delivered them to you (1 Cor 11:2 RSV).

For "traditions" is, once again, the English translation of *paradosis* and it means, once again, not merely written but extra-biblical tradition as well. Precisely what Paul does *not* do is give the Corinthians the slightest indication that his writings alone are the word of God or that they will someday contain everything he has delivered extra-biblically. Nowhere does he say, "Look sharp, guys! One of these days we'll crystallize what we're saying into a complete New Testament, but until then just stick with the clunky and unreliable tradition we gave you." On the contrary, he praises them for remembering his *paradosis,* which has *already been handed on to them before his letters were written,* and urges them to stick to both his letters *and* this extra-biblical tradition. Thus, in Corinth as in Thessalonica, the total *paradosis* — Scripture and Tradition — is the word of God. It is on *this* word, not the Scripture alone, that these churches are founded.

This was confirmed by the Acts of the Apostles. After all, Acts is an extended portrait of a living community of saints propagating itself by handing on a largely oral *paradosis.* It does not show apostles churning out inspired writings on which to build churches (though a few of them occasionally do write things). For a Bible-based Evangelical like me, the interesting thing about the apostles, evangelists, prophets, and teachers in Acts is what they *don't* spend much time doing: they don't spend much time writing the Bible.

Now, to be sure, when they do put quill to papyrus they teach their churches to regard this too as authoritative; "not as the word of men, but as it actually is, the word of God" (2 Th 2:13). However, these words have authority not because they are written but because they are *apostolic.* The apostles knew that Christ had told them "He who listens to you listens to me." So they wrote as they spoke — with the authority of Christ. But they mostly spoke. Indeed, as I read the Acts of the Apostles, I was struck by the fact that the "word" it refers to virtually always meant the word of oral *paradosis.*

My Evangelical friends were certain I was wrong about this one. "The apostles are *constantly* quoting Scripture," they said. "From Peter's quotation of Joel and Psalm 16 on Pentecost to

Paul's preaching in Pisidian Antioch you have a message that is steeped in Scripture. Even the Thessalonians did not receive some non-biblical 'tradition' as you suppose. For Acts *tells* us what Paul taught them 'by word of mouth.' He 'reasoned with them from the Scriptures, explaining and proving that the Christ had to suffer and rise from the dead' " (Acts 17:2-3).

My friends continued: "Scripture commends the churches for doing likewise. Take the Bereans, for instance. Acts says clearly:

> Now the Bereans were of more noble charac-
> ter than the Thessalonians, for they received
> the message with great eagerness and exam-
> ined the Scriptures every day to see if what
> Paul said was true (Acts 17:11).

"Clearly then, it is untrue that the apostles founded their churches on a tradition. The Church was founded on nothing other than the Scriptures themselves."

My own Evangelical bones told me I should believe this. To be sure, I certainly did not deny that the apostles quoted Scripture (whatever their canon was), regarded it as the inspired word of God, and encouraged their disciples to know it. This was all true.

But it was also beside the point. As I read Acts, I was compelled to admit that where my friends saw the apostles founding the Church on the Bible, I saw the apostles founding the Church on their *paradosis* of Jesus Christ. Then, as it was appropriate, they called on the Old Testament Scripture to act as a *witness* to that Tradition.

What, after all, do the early churches *receive* from the apostles? Not primarily the Old Testament; like the Jews who stoned Stephen, the early Christians already *had* that. No, they receive instead a Tradition — mostly oral and occasionally written — about a *new* and *final* revelation that was, as Paul says, "not made known to men in other generations as it has now been revealed by the Spirit to God's holy apostles and prophets" (Eph 3:5). Indeed, one of the constant refrains of the New Testament writers is the need for the completion of Scripture by the *paradosis* of Christ. That is why Paul insists that we cannot hope to see the true meaning of the Jewish Scriptures apart from the revelation of Christ himself. They remain, says Paul, "veiled" until the *paradosis* he *preaches* comes to take the veil away by the power of the Spirit (2 Cor 3:14).

According to Paul, the new revelation was not revealed through the Old Testament writings; it was *hidden* in them. What *revealed* the new revelation was Christ Jesus, who *is* the new revelation. And what revealed Christ Jesus was not primarily Scripture but those persons he had chosen to proclaim him: the apostles whose proclamation became the Tradition and the Scripture of which Paul spoke.

This seemed to me to clearly be the implication of the very passages my friends cited from Acts. Nobody in Acts — not Stephen, Peter, Paul, or the Bereans — ever sits down with his Jewish Bible and *derives* the gospel from it as we derive a conclusion from a set of premises in a math problem. Nobody grabs a copy of Isaiah or Deuteronomy, does a topical Bible study, and arrives at the conclusion that Messiah will be handed over for crucifixion, rise from the dead, bestow his Spirit on the Church at Pentecost, call the Gentiles into a covenant with him, and promise to come again in glory to judge the living and the dead. Quite the contrary: nobody, before these things actually happen, sees them coming, *especially* the apostles. As the Apostle John observed, until Jesus opened their eyes — by his death and resurrection and not a Bible study — "they still did not understand from Scripture that Jesus had to rise from the dead," even when they stood at the very mouth of the empty tomb (Jn 20:9).

That is why nobody in the length and breadth of the New Testament talks as though he figured the new revelation out from Scripture. Rather, most speak of understanding Scripture as the Ethiopian eunuch did: "How can I, unless someone explains it to me?" (Acts 8:31). And for the eunuch as for the rest of the New Testament hearers, the explanation comes, not from further Bible study, but from the apostolic *paradosis* of Jesus Christ which "utters things hidden since the creation of the world" (Mt 13:35).

That is why Paul never says that the gospel is based on or derived from the Law and the Prophets. Rather, he declares that the Law and the Prophets "testify" to the righteousness revealed in Christ "apart from law" (Rom 3:21). The Law and the Prophets point to Christ. They are signs of him. They *bear witness* to him. But he is also truly *hidden* in them until God, through the oral and written *paradosis* of his holy apostles, reveals Christ and his gift of righteousness.

Thus, in Paul's thought, as in Acts, the Church is not founded on Scripture; rather, Scripture is called to *bear witness* to the apostolic *paradosis*, and it is this *paradosis* which both founds the Church and focuses the light of Scripture.

Perhaps the plainest example of this apostolic habit of mind occurs in 1 Peter 1:23-25 which speaks of the "living and enduring word of God." Note carefully how the text reads here, for many people assume that it is speaking of the inspiration of the Old Testament. After all, he quotes Isaiah 40:7-8 saying:

> The grass withers and the flowers fall,
> but the word of the Lord remains forever.

Yet when I looked again, I noticed something remarkable. Peter is *not* identifying the verses from Isaiah as the living and enduring word of God. Strange as it seemed to my Bible-only Evangelical ears, he was, like Paul, *calling Isaiah as a witness to his own preached apostolic message of Christ*. For Peter, the living and enduring word of God is not only the written word of Scripture; it is "the word that has been proclaimed to you" — that is, the apostolic Tradition of God.

So in sharp contrast to the notion that the apostolic churches were founded on the Bible alone, the scenario is really this:

Christ reveals himself (much to the astonishment of the apostles and everyone else) and then, only *after* he has fulfilled the new revelation hidden in the Old Testament, does he remind his disciples that he has fulfilled it.

> "How foolish you are, and how slow of heart to believe all that the prophets have spoken! Did not the Christ have to suffer these things and then enter his glory?" And beginning with Moses and all the Prophets, he explained to them what was said in all the Scriptures concerning himself (Lk 24:25-27).

This passage hardly indicates that the apostles arrived at the gospel from a deductive Scripture lesson. They did not use a *Thompson Chain Reference Bible* on the Emmaus Road and conclude that Jesus must be risen. Rather, the Risen Christ *appeared* to them and practically had to rub their noses in the Scripture they had been reading all their lives before they finally began to see his gospel and himself concealed there.

The picture of the Church given in Acts is remarkably similar to the picture of the Catholic Church drawn by the Second Vatican Council. In apostolic times, as today, "Sacred Tradition and Sacred Scripture form one sacred deposit of the word of God."[9] Thus the Christians in Acts persevere, not only in Bible study like the Bereans, but in the "apostles' teaching" (Acts 2:42). This includes, then as now, the apostolic prayers, preaching, baptism, breaking of the bread, and laying on of hands, among other things. Thus, Paul has "discussions with them from the scriptures" in Thessalonica because they are the *witness to* the Tradition of "this Jesus I am proclaiming to you" (Acts 17:3), not the source of it. Thus, the Bereans see Christ in the Scriptures they have read all their lives precisely because they see them through the lens of Paul's *paradosis*.

The apostolic "word" in the New Testament — that word upon which every Church from Jerusalem to Rome is founded

— is then a Tradition both of letter and *word*. "The faith that was once for all entrusted" was entrusted, not to a book, but to a living community of apostles and their disciples — "the saints," as Jude 3 says. And according to the Catholic Church, that Tradition has been "handed on, as it were from hand to hand, from the apostles under the inspiration of the Holy Spirit"[10] right down to the present — handed down in a Tradition both written and unwritten.

But I hesitated. It was apparently handed down with a lot of impurities by a merely human church. After all, I thought, don't devotion to Mary, adoration of the Eucharist, and the so-called "Sacrifice of the Mass" testify clearly enough to that?

It seemed to me that for all the strengths of the Catholic view of Tradition and for all the concessions I was forced to make to it, nonetheless it still looked as though all sorts of unbiblical traditions had crept in after the apostles were gone. Worse still, it appeared that the authority of the Church to promulgate these traditions was the Church itself. If so, wasn't that reasoning just as circular as our Evangelical reliance on the Bible alone?

Which got me thinking again.

NOTES

1. Second Vatican Council, *Dogmatic Constitution on Divine Revelation*, II, 9.
2. *Dogmatic Constitution on Divine Revelation*, III, 12.
3. *Dogmatic Constitution on Divine Revelation*, III, 11.
4. *Dogmatic Constitution on Divine Revelation*, II, 8.
5. Council of Trent, *Decree on Sacred Scripture and Tradition*: Denziger 783 (1501).
6. *Dogmatic Constitution on Divine Revelation*, II, 9.
7. For example, Paul knows Jesus is a Jew of David's line (Rom 1:3); that John the Baptist was his forerunner and had disavowed any claim to his own Messiah-ship (Acts 13:24-25); that his chief disciples were Peter, James, and

John (Gal 2:9); that he had predicted his return "like a thief" (1 Thes 5:4); that he had instituted the Eucharist (1 Cor 11:23-25); that he had been rejected by the Jewish leaders (1 Thes 2:15), tried under Pontius Pilate (1 Tm 5:13), and crucified for us (Gal 3:1); that he was laid in a tomb (Acts 13:29); that he had been raised from the dead and seen by many witnesses (1 Cor 15:3-8); and that he had ascended (Eph 4:9-10).

8. *The Jerome Biblical Commentary*, Vol. 2, Raymond E. Brown, S.S., Joseph A. Fitzmeyer, S.J., Roland E. Murphy, O. Carm., eds. (Englewood Cliffs: Prentice-Hall, 1968), p. 804; Gordon D. Fee, *The New International Commentary on the New Testament*, The First Epistle to the Corinthians (Grand Rapids: W. B. Eerdmans Publishing Company, 1987), p. 449, n. 29; James H. Moulton and George Milligan, *The Vocabulary of the Greek New Testament Illustrated From the Papyri and Other Non-literary Sources* (London: Hodder and Stoughton, 1930), p. 483.

9. *Dogmatic Constitution on Divine Revelation*, II, 10.

10. *Decree on Sacred Scripture and Tradition*: Denziger 783 (1501).

Chapter Eight
Circles and Lines

Thou art the man! — The Prophet Nathan (2 Sm 12:7)

Was the Catholic reliance on Sacred Tradition really as circular as our Evangelical belief in the self-attesting Bible? And did this reliance really lead to false doctrines?

It seemed to me that this *might* be so, but I had seen many of my assumptions about the Catholic view of tradition explode in my face already. I had imagined Scripture was self-attesting; I had discovered otherwise. I had assumed Christ and his apostles had no use for tradition as revelation; I had discovered otherwise. I had imagined we Evangelicals had no reliance on tradition as revelation; I had discovered otherwise. I had imagined the Church was founded on the Bible alone; I had discovered otherwise.

Therefore, though I was wary, I was no longer ready to reject Catholic teaching out of hand — especially since there was no mistaking where the road of my own "Bible only" theology led. What, I wondered, would it profit me to gain the Bible alone and lose my soul to modernism? The problem was clear: saying that Scripture was the sole source of revelation was saying that some of the most basic dogmas and ethics of the Faith were permanently up for grabs. It was indeed saying that the whole case for the Faith must forever remain a chain of logic links attached to a hook hanging from a nail hammered firmly into nothing. In the end, the claim of Bible-only revelation really did leave me with R.C. Sproul's "fallible collection of infallible books," and with an Evangelicalism naked before the onslaught of modernism. If Sacred Tradition is not revelation, then the Heisenberg Uncertainty Principle must henceforth be the Evangelical creed and "What is truth?" the inscription on its tomb. In seeking to save my Bible-only life I could only lose it.

Yet what if I were willing to lose my Bible-only life in the hope of saving it? This unsettling thought looked to me like the only game in town. So I swallowed my anxiety and turned to look again at just what the Catholic Church claimed to be handing down.

I began with the question of how tradition, according to Catholic teaching, came down to us. "Is it," I asked, "just as circular for the Church to say 'Our inspired tradition is from the apostles' as for a modern Evangelical to say 'Scripture is self-attesting'?"

"No," said the Church, "it is not circular at all. For the authority of the Church's bishops to say this comes not from themselves nor from their own claims, but from the apostles who appointed them and ordered them to appoint others in their name." As the Second Vatican Council put it:

> In order that the full and living Gospel might
> always be preserved in the Church the Apostles
> left bishops as their successors. They gave them
> "their own position of teaching authority."[1]

According to Catholic teaching, the Church's authority was a line, not a circle. That line, said the Church, led straight back via the bishops to the apostles, and through them, to Jesus Christ. Furthermore the Church said that the evidence for the beginning of this line is in the New Testament itself, while the evidence for Bible-only revelation is (as I had discovered) simply nowhere in Scripture.

I tested the Church's claim in light of the New Testament

documents. Beginning with the gospels I saw a picture of authority delegated first by the Father to the Son and then by the Son to the Twelve ("He who receives you receives me, and he who receives me receives the one who sent me" [Mt 10:40]). So far, so good. But was there evidence of a corresponding delegation of Spirit-led authority by the Twelve to others after them, as the Catholic Church said, or did the line of authority die with the Apostle John around 90 A.D.?

I looked through Acts again and saw numerous indications that it did not die. For wherever the apostles founded churches, they did indeed delegate successors to govern in their place.[2] According to the New Testament, these successors have authority, not merely to preach but to *command*, to render authoritative judgment on whether a doctrine agrees with apostolic teaching (1 Tm 1:3), and even to discipline unruly members of the Body (1 Tm 5:20). Thus, when the fracas over circumcision develops, it is "the apostles and the elders" who meet at the Council of Jerusalem to discern the mind of Christ (Acts 15:6). One of their chief complaints against the circumcision party? Not that they acted without authority from Scripture, but that they "went out from us without our authorization" (Acts 15:24). Likewise, it is not merely the apostles but "the elders" who promulgate their decision with full apostolic authority expressed in the words, "'it seemed good to the Holy Spirit and to *us*. . . .'" (Act 15:23;28).

In short, these apostolic delegates are delegated apostolic *authority*. In turn, they are under one overriding obligation to the apostles: "*Guard* yourselves and all the flock of which the Holy Spirit has made you overseers" (Acts 20:28). "So be on your *guard*" (Acts 20:31). "*Guard* what has been entrusted to your care" (1 Tm 6:20). "*Guard* the good deposit that was entrusted to you — *guard* it with the help of the Holy Spirit who lives in us" (2 Tm 1:14).

What exactly is to be guarded? Well, the flock and its Scriptures certainly. That is why Timothy is commended for knowing the Holy Scriptures and commanded to use them for "teaching, rebuking, correcting and training in righteousness" (2 Tm 3:16). But is that all the apostolic delegate is to guard?

No. Paul explicitly and repeatedly commands him to guard, not only the letter, but the unwritten apostolic *word* as well. Thus he tells Timothy, "what you *HEARD* from me, keep as the pattern of sound teaching, with faith and love in Christ Jesus" (2 Tm 1:13). Likewise, he commands Timothy to adhere closely, not only to his letters but to "things you have *heard me say* in the presence of many witnesses" (2 Tm 2:2). In other words, the apostolic successor is under solemn obligation to preserve the entire *paradosis*, whether he received it by word of mouth or by letter. Moreover, Paul goes on in the same verse to say that Timothy must himself pass on this written and unwritten tradition to "reliable men who will also be qualified to teach others" (2 Tm 2:2). Similarly, he commands Titus to appoint successors whose job, once again, is to "teach what is in accord with sound doctrine" (Ti 2:1).

And apparently, Timothy, Titus, and the many other apostolic successors in the various churches did just this. For in the years immediately following the apostles, we find that the various post-apostolic communities are in fact governed by a series of successors who regard their task as being precisely the thing Paul said it was: guarding the good deposit entrusted to them and, as the Church grew, themselves appointing successors with the help of the Holy Spirit.

Thus Irenaeus writes in France (about 180):

> It is possible, then, for everyone in every Church, who may wish to know the truth, to contemplate the tradition of the Apostles which has been made known throughout the whole world. And we are in a position to enumerate those who were instituted bishops by the Apostles, and their successors to our own times; men who neither knew nor taught anything like these heretics[3] rave about. For if the Apostles

had known hidden mysteries which they taught to the elite secretly and apart from the rest, they would have handed them down especially to those very ones to whom they were committing the self-same churches. For surely they wished all those and their successors to be perfect and without reproach, to whom they handed on their authority.[4]

To prove that the line of apostolic successors can indeed be traced, Irenaeus picks out one church as an example. The Church he picks is Rome.

The blessed Apostles [Peter and Paul], having founded and built up the Church [of Rome], they handed over the office of the episcopate to Linus. Paul makes mention of this Linus in the Epistle to Timothy. To him succeeded Anacletus; and after him, in the third place from the Apostles, Clement was chosen for the episcopate. . . . To this Clement, Evaristus succeeded; and Alexander succeeded Evaristus. Then, sixth after the Apostles, Sixtus was appointed; after him, Telesphorus, who was gloriously martyred. Then Hyginus; after him, Pius; and after him, Anicetus. Soter succeeded Anicetus, and now, in the twelfth place after the Apostles, the lot of the episcopate has fallen to Eleutherus. In this order, and by the teaching of the Apostles handed down in the Church, the preaching of the truth has come down to us.[5]

This process of apostolic succession is verified by the very Clement of whom Irenaeus speaks. Around the year 80, even before the Apostle John has died, Clement, who was "in the third place from the Apostles," writes:

The Apostles received the gospel for us from the Lord Jesus Christ; and Jesus Christ was sent from God. Christ, therefore, is from God, and the Apostles are from Christ. Both of these orderly arrangements, then, are by God's will. Receiving their instructions and being full of confidence on account of the resurrection of our Lord Jesus Christ, and confirmed in faith by the word of God, they went forth in the complete assurance of the Holy Spirit, preaching the good news that the Kingdom of God is coming. *Through countryside and city they preached; and they appointed their earliest converts, testing them by the Spirit, to be the bishops and deacons of future believers*[6] [italics added].

Further, Clement confirms that the apostles desired their authority be handed down in perpetuity. He adds:

Our Apostles knew through our Lord Jesus Christ that there would be strife for the office of bishop. For this reason, therefore, having received perfect foreknowledge, they appointed those who have already been mentioned, *and afterwards added the further provision that, if they should die, other approved men should succeed to their ministry*[7] [italics added].

Because of this direct delegation of apostolic authority, yet another early Christian — Ignatius — writes (about 110): "You must all follow the bishop as Jesus Christ follows the Father, and the presbytery as you would the Apostles."[8]

Very well, then. Judging from the historical data, the Catholic picture of apostolic succession appeared to be sound. We do indeed have a solid picture, both in the New Testament and in writings immediately after it, of the apostles ordaining a line of successors rooted in the authority Christ himself had given them when he told them to make disciples of all nations.

But the question remained: what about all these apparently unbiblical Catholic traditions? Clement, Ignatius, and Irenaeus believed a lot of rather questionable stuff, as far as I could see. Clement, for instance, taught that the bishops offered sacrifices (evidently referring to the Sacrifice of the Mass).[9] Ignatius likewise appeared to have gone off the deep end with his insistence that Eucharist is quite literally "the Flesh of our Savior Jesus Christ, Flesh which suffered for our sins and which the Father, in his goodness, raised up again."[10] Irenaeus regarded Mary as the "Second Eve" and said that she, "being obedient, was made the cause of salvation for herself and for the whole human race." None of this was clear from Scripture and some of it did not seem to be mentioned in Scripture at all. . . .

I stopped short, struck suddenly by my own words. "Unbiblical." "Not mentioned in Scripture." I had used such words many times in my critique of Catholic tradition. Yet what did I *mean* by them?

Did I mean that a tradition not explicit in Scripture was necessarily opposed to Scripture? No, for the ban on abortion and polygamy is not explicit in Scripture, yet we Evangelicals believed right along with the early Church that Christianity was fundamentally opposed to abortion and we found our belief to be quite amicable to Scripture. Likewise, for we Evangelicals believed in the Tradition of the Closure of Public Revelation, used terms like "Trinity" and practiced things like "altar calls" and "asking Jesus Christ into your heart as your personal Lord and Savior" — even though such doctrine and phraseology is as apparently absent from Scripture as the idea of Mary as "cause of salvation." Indeed, as we have seen, we very obviously believed that the canon of Scripture itself, though nowhere mentioned in Scripture, was authoritative.

So what *did* I mean by the term "unbiblical"?

As I thought about it, I realized I meant not *extra-biblical*, but *anti-biblical*. The Evangelical practices and doctrines mentioned above, while not actually mentioned in Scripture, were not *hostile* to Scripture. They were extra-biblical, but not anti-biblical. Moreover, different levels of importance attached to such traditions. Some of them, such as altar calls, were small "t" traditions not essential to the Faith; they were just a workable way of enacting it which could be changed if necessary. But other traditions, like the canon of Scripture and the doctrine of the Trinity, clearly were big "T" Tradition which could not be changed without destroying the Faith root and branch.

But I also realized that what's sauce for the goose is sauce for the gander. If we Evangelicals could hold a Big T extra-biblical Tradition like the canon of Scripture or the closure of public revelation to be revelation handed down from the apostles, why did I automatically assume that Clement's, Ignatius', and Irenaeus's extra-biblical traditions were anti-biblical? To be sure, they *might* be. But I had not proven this simply by asserting that these traditions were extra-biblical. I had merely assumed it (as I had once assumed that all tradition was human tradition).

So I began to think about the post-apostolic Fathers and their extra-biblical traditions.

At my church we had believed (without giving it a great deal of thought) that these Catholic-sounding doctrines and others like them were the result of paganism creeping into the Church after the apostles had died. I had long had a vague picture of a gaggle of semi-converted Roman yahoos and ultra-intellectual Greek wise guys all sitting down with the pure biblical gospel not long after the Apostle John died and injecting their little superstitions and philosophies in an effort to make the high and hard truth of Scripture more appealing to their Greco-Roman sensibilities. Thus the worship of Isis and Athena transmogrified at their hands into Irenaeus's devotion to Mary as the "Second Eve" and "cause of salvation" (a notion which will form the basis of the later Catholic formulations about Mary as "co-mediatrix"). Similarly, I believed that Ignatius, like a typical half-pagan, took John 6 so literally that he imported odd Mithraic ideas about ritual blood feasts, giving us the notion of "the Body and Blood of Christ." And so on for purgatory, relics, and prayers to the dead.

As I once said to a friend, "That's what happens when you have two thousand years to suppress scriptural truth and add a bunch of pagan gunk."

But now I thought again about the tradition of monogamy — Basil the Great and his fellow Christian leaders and their remarkably Dr. Dobson-like stand against polygamy in spite of its ongoing acceptance among pagans. Strange behavior for a Church capitulating to paganism.

I wondered, what did I actually *know* about these early Christians? Truth to tell, very little.

So the next question was obvious: *were* these early Christian bishops hostile to the Gospel and eager to alter it to their own quasi-pagan purposes? As I began to read their writings and the accounts of their lives, the impression became clearer and clearer that, if they were, they had a funny way of showing it.

Consider, first of all, the preservation of Scripture itself.

Everything we have said about the honesty of the scriptural authors in *writing* the gospel account is also true of the post-apostolic Church in *preserving* it. This is shown not only by what the early Church *did* in preserving these texts, but by what it did *not* do. It never set out to alter them even when numerous voices in the early centuries of Christianity, both inside and outside the Church, seized upon various embarrassing verses to "prove" that Jesus was not God. All those nettlesome texts where Jesus is described as unable to do something (Mk 6:5), or is surprised (Mt 8:10), or declares his ignorance (Mt 24:36), or asks questions (evidently because he really doesn't know the answer) (Lk 8:45), or exclaims "'Why do you call me good?'" (Mk 10:18), or cries out in anguish, "'My God, my God, why have you forsaken me?'" (Mk 15:34; Mt 27:46) — all those texts provided ammunition for nonbelievers who attacked the ordinary teaching of the bishops that Jesus is God in human flesh. Yet the post-apostolic bishops *never* repudiated these texts as false interpolations or papered them over as the Jesus Seminar says they papered over the merely human rabbi with divinizing myths. Instead they fully embraced these hard sayings as part of the essential story and defended them as the very word of God. Why would they do this if they were so breezily ready to do whatever it took to ignore Scripture and impose their own traditions?

But even more difficult for my Pagan Creep theory is the fact that the early Church did not take it lying down when a second-century heretic named Marcion organized the very first canon of New Testament Scripture in the history of Christendom—a canon which really *did* attempt to suppress Scripture, snip out all the inconveniences from the gospels and add a bunch of pagan gunk.

Marcion held that the Old Testament was entirely defunct, that the Jewish God was a bad god and that Jesus Christ was the good God (a pure spirit being who only appeared to be human). Marcion's great hero was Paul, but he taught that various sinister influences had inserted false Jewish interpolations into Paul's writings (which Marcion obligingly deleted). For the same reason he rejected the rest of the documents which would later be collated to constitute the New Testament as well as all the gospels but Luke (which he edited heavily to suit his theories). Essentially, Marcion wanted very badly to create a gospel that would fit in with the latest fashionable theories of pagan Gnosticism and get as far away as possible from Jewish Scripture. That is, he really did what I thought the early Catholic Church had wanted to do.

So what was the response of the early Church I had thought was all agog for suppressing scriptural truth and importing paganism as quickly as possible? Did they seize on Marcion's ideas as the perfect means of severing the Faith from its Jewish roots and alloying Christianity with the human traditions of the Greco-Roman world? Did they lazily dally with Marcion's ideas in order to attract a few more people enamored of Gnostic teachings? On the contrary, in the delicate words of Tertullian (c. 210), the early Church Fathers agreed that Marcion had "a pumpkin . . . in place of a brain"[11] and denounced him furiously.

Surely, I thought, this too is strange behavior for a Church eager to abandon Scripture. But if this was odd, then odder still was the fact that one of the Fathers responded to Marcion's attack on Scripture by vigorously asserting a "counter-canon" that not only reaffirmed the Old Testament pretty much as we have it today, but largely resembled our present New Testament as well. That Father was Irenaeus, who not only reiterates a canon counter to Marcion, but vigorously asserts the apostolic origin of the New Testament books in that canon by writing:

> Matthew also issued among the Hebrews a written Gospel in their own language, while Peter and Paul were evangelizing in Rome and laying the foundation of the Church. After their departure, Mark, the disciple and interpreter of Peter, also handed down to us in writing what had been preached by Peter. Luke also, the companion of Paul, set down in a book the Gospel preached by him. Afterwards, John, the disciple of the Lord who reclined at his bosom, also published a Gospel, while he was residing at Ephesus in Asia.[12]

Now the fascinating thing for me was that virtually all of this is extra-biblical tradition (recall that no gospel writer gives his name), yet this testimony of Irenaeus is the very thing upon which we Evangelicals build our belief that Matthew is from Matthew, Luke from Luke, Mark from Mark, and John from John. It is on men like Irenaeus that we Evangelicals base our complete trust that Mark preserves the teaching of Peter and Luke the teaching of Paul.[13]

And rightly so by all rules of normal historical research. Irenaeus's testimony is frequently corroborated by other post-apostolic writers and roundly endorsed by the early Church. Papias (c. 130) for example, also bears witness to the Church's memory in his "Explanation of the Sayings of the Lord" that Mark was a disciple of Peter's and that he "wrote down accurately whatever he remembered" and "made it his concern to omit nothing that he had heard nor to falsify anything therein."[14] Likewise Justin Martyr describes the Gospels as the "Memoirs of the Apostles."[15]

Equally significant is just how these early Fathers claim to know these things. They say they know it through their bishops — descended from the apostles in exactly the way prescribed by Paul in his letters to Timothy and Titus — who have preserved the apostolic *paradosis*, both in word and letter. As Irenaeus elsewhere stresses:

> It is necessary to obey those who are the presbyters in the Church, those who, as we have shown, have succession from the Apostles; those who have received, with the succession of the episcopate, the sure charism of truth according to the good pleasure of the Father.[16]

In short, the Church immediately following the apostles believes that the apostles acted under the inspiration of God *not only in writing the Scriptures but in creating the office of bishop to succeed them when they die*. Both the Scriptures and the bishops are intended to provide for the future; upon both rests the "charism of truth." By both these means, united and inseparable, the full *paradosis* of Scripture and Tradition is to be handed down with neither addition nor subtraction. The very earliest bishops received this *paradosis*, not from some self-imposed delusion of grandeur, but from the lips of the apostles themselves and *in the presence of many witnesses*. That is why Irenaeus later proudly records this anecdote about his own mentor, Polycarp:

Polycarp, however, was instructed not only by the Apostles, and conversed with many who had seen Christ, but was also appointed bishop of the Church in Smyrna, by the Apostles in Asia. I saw him in my early youth; for he tarried a long time, and when quite old he departed this life in a glorious and most noble martyrdom. He always taught those things which he had learned from the Apostles, and which the Church had handed down, and which are true. *To these things all the Churches in Asia bear witness, as do also the successors of Polycarp even to the present time*[17] [italics added].

Irenaeus is thoroughly devoted to the gospel Polycarp learned from the apostles. Arch-conservative to the bone, he dreads the thought of corrupting it by either addition to or subtraction from the gospel. That is why he writes books like *Adversus Haereses* or (as he called it) "Detection and Overthrow of the Gnosis Falsely So-Called." Irenaeus's whole purpose in writing this book was to prevent any trace of anti-biblical teaching from creeping into the apostolic *paradosis*. For the same reason, he remonstrates with a Christian-turned-Gnostic named Florinus precisely for embracing such quasi-paganism:

These doctrines, Florinus, to put it mildly, are not of sound judgment. These doctrines are not in accord with the Church, and they involve those who accept them in the greatest of impiety. These doctrines were not handed down to you by the presbyters who came before us and who were the companions of the Apostles.[18]

He then venerates the memory of his beloved Polycarp with these very significant words:

> I remember the events of those days better than the ones of recent years. What a boy learns grows with the mind and becomes a part of him, so that I am able to describe the very place in which the blessed Polycarp sat as he discoursed, his goings and his comings, the manner of his life, his physical appearance, as well as the discourses he delivered to the people, and how he spoke of his familiar conversation with John and with the rest of those who had seen the Lord, and how he would recall their words to mind. All that he had heard from them concerning the Lord or about His miracles and about His teaching, having received it from eyewitnesses of the Word of Life, Polycarp related in harmony with the Scriptures.[19]

This Polycarp whom Irenaeus so reveres is then a man who actually heard the Apostle John with his own ears and who spoke with him in "familiar conversation." In addition, he is an apostolic successor, universally respected in the early Church, who went on to become bishop of Smyrna, a church community for which Christ has nothing but praise (Rev 2:8-11). Further, Polycarp was heroic in his defense of the Faith, strongly opposing Marcion and his bogus Bible:

> Once he was met by Marcion, who said to him,
> "Do you recognize me?" and Polycarp replied,
> "I recognize you as the firstborn of Satan!"[20]

As in life, so in death. Polycarp eventually chose to be burned to death for his faith in Christ rather than compromise with paganism in any way. As the *Martyrdom of Polycarp* records (written by eyewitnesses shortly after the event):

> When the Proconsul urged him and said, "Take

> the oath and I will release you; revile Christ,"
> Polycarp answered: "Eighty-six years I have
> served Him, and He has never done me wrong.
> How, then, should I be able to blaspheme my
> King who has saved me?"[21]

Thus we have in Polycarp a martyr for the Faith, a pillar of orthodoxy, a friend of the Apostle John's, and a highly venerated member of the Church who drove deep into Irenaeus's being the conviction that the true things he heard from the very lips of the apostles as well as from their Scriptures must at all costs be preserved against compromise.

So what, according to Irenaeus, *are* the true things which he learned from Polycarp and Polycarp learned directly from the lips of John and died a martyr to proclaim? Well, in addition to the proclamation of Scripture that Christ is the only begotten Son of God, crucified for our sins and raised to life for our justification, Irenaeus tells us he has it as sound doctrine that Mary:

> being obedient, was made the cause of salva-
> tion for herself and for the whole human
> race. . . . Thus, the knot of Eve's disobedience
> was loosed by the obedience of Mary. What
> the virgin Eve had bound in unbelief, the Vir-
> gin Mary loosed through faith.[22]

In short, Irenaeus is adamant that the tradition of Mary as the Second Eve and "cause of salvation" comes, not from paganism (which he loathes) nor from his own fancy, nor from an aberration of Polycarp, but from the Apostle John himself. Such things, says Irenaeus, though not explicit in Scripture, are nonetheless in harmony with it and are, in fact, an integral part of the gospel John preached.

Of course, an Evangelical like me naturally demanded to know just how this tradition concerning Mary could possibly be reconciled with Scripture. After all, Paul clearly says there is "one mediator between God and men, the man Christ Jesus" (1 Tm 2:5). So Irenaeus and Polycarp, for all their impressive credentials, looked pretty anti-biblical to me. But as I researched further I discovered looks had been deceiving me. What I found, in a nutshell, was this:

Jesus *is* the one mediator. He is also the one Teacher and the one Son of God (Mt 24:10; Jn 1:14). But that oneness, according to Scripture, is the oneness of *primacy*, not of exclusiveness. He *shares* these roles with his followers by grace so that, as he said, "Anyone who has faith in me will do what I have been doing. He will do even greater things than these, because I am going to the Father" (Jn 14:12). Thus Jesus, the one Teacher, commands *us* to teach (Mt 28:20) and Jesus, the one Son of God, commands *us* to pray "Our Father" (Mt 6:9). Likewise, Jesus, the one mediator, makes *us* a holy priesthood (that is, mediators) between God and man (1 Pt 2:5) and commands us to intercede for one another and to give our lives for one another in his Spirit (1 Tm 2:1; Jn 15:12-13). So there is nothing anti-biblical about co-mediation. All Christians are co-mediators to one degree or another.

Therefore, so was Mary. But Mary was something more: she was "highly favored" as Gabriel said and "blessed . . . among women" in the words of Elizabeth (Lk 1:28; 42). Indeed, by virtue of God's unique favor she became even more blessed and pivotal than Eve. For as Irenaeus notes, she chose the opposite of Eve: she chose to say yes to God.

Eve, the Mother of All the Living, long ago became the Mother of All the Dying by her disobedience. Similarly, on Mary's obedience, as on Eve's disobedience, hung the fate of our race. In saying yes to God, Mary was not a tool but a person; not a robot but "God's fellow worker" (1 Cor 3:9). And her choice, like Eve's, had profound significance, not just for her, but for all of us. For as Eve said yes not merely to her own death, but to the death of us all, so Mary said yes, not merely to the birth of a man, but to the rebirth of the whole human race in him whom she knew to be "Son of the Most High" (Lk 1:32). Thus, in saying yes to the Incarnation, Mary said yes to being our Mother through the Second Adam, just as Eve became our Mother through the First Adam. Or as Irenaeus put it, Mary was "made the cause of salvation for herself and for the whole human race." Yet she was made so, not because she is a goddess, but because it was God who worked in her to will and to act according to his good pleasure (Phil 2:13). This is why Irenaeus says that Mary did all this "through faith," not on her own. And Irenaeus's grandfather in the Faith looks a great deal as though he concurs. For John's gospel makes special note of the fact that the dying Christ says to the Beloved Disciple (who is an image of the Church), "Behold, your mother" and to his mother, "here is your son" (Jn 19:26-27).

Thus, spooky as Irenaeus's words sounded at first, I was eventually forced to concede that they did indeed harmonize with Scripture rather well. Indeed, the more I studied, the more it seemed to me the tradition Irenaeus cited concerning Mary focused the light of Scripture in an unexpectedly satisfying and sensible way, much as the Church's tradition concerning monogamy and abortion did. And most amazingly, such tradition was rooted, not in centuries of inventiveness, but in a few decades of stodgy arch-conservatism courtesy of Polycarp and Irenaeus.

At this, I recalled my crack about "two thousand years of pagan gunk" and realized for the first time a problem with my reasoning: men like Irenaeus, Polycarp, Ignatius, and Clement didn't *have* two thousand years to add pagan gunk. They wrote anywhere from ten years before to ninety years after the death of the Apostle John, and often well within the lifetime of the many thousands of devoted disciples who had heard the apostles with their own ears. This was brought home to me by the witness of Irenaeus — the very same witness who, as we have seen, is one of our principal sources for the veracity of the gospels and who fought paganism tooth and nail. For Irenaeus regards Clement of Rome, as much as Luke or

Mark, as a faithful guardian of the apostolic teaching. Yet this Clement who, like Polycarp, "had seen the blessed Apostles and was acquainted with them"[23] speaks of yet another doctrine which I thought had been imported from paganism: the Sacrifice of the Mass.[24]

To realize the implications of this, we must recall that this Clement is writing about 80 A.D., well before the Apostle John dies. Moreover, he is writing to the Church at Corinth, just across the Aegean Sea from Ephesus, where John has been contending for the purity of the Faith for many years. Thus, Clement's writing about the "sacrifices" offered by the overseers, challenged my Pagan Creep theory. For that theory had to explain how a "simple memorial meal" of communion was suddenly transformed into the wholly alien Sacrifice of the Mass while John was still alive and quite ready to kick heresy at home and abroad — a fact fully demonstrated by his vigorous awareness and denunciation of various errors in churches all over Asia Minor preserved in 1 John and the book of Revelation. Just as Paul kept his finger on the pulse of the various churches dotted all over the world even when he was in prison, so John was evidently well-supplied with news of his flock via a Church that was, as they say, "well-networked." So he kept a close watch on them, especially when he was far away.

One would expect, then, that some complaint about Clement's supposed perversion of the Faith would find its way into John's writings or, failing that, into his preaching to men such as Polycarp. Indeed, if Clement's teaching is as foreign to the apostolic mind as I had supposed, one can hardly imagine John's and Polycarp's angry opposition to such newfangled doctrine *not* exerting as strong an influence on Irenaeus as their bitter opposition to Marcion and the Gnostics did. For Irenaeus gives eloquent testimony to Polycarp's horror at the thought of novel ideas polluting the gospel:

> I am able to bear witness in the presence of
> God that if that blessed and apostolic old man

had heard any such thing, he would have cried
out and stopped his ears; and, as was his custom, he would have said, "O good God, to what
times you have spared me, that I should endure these things!" He would have fled away
from the place where, sitting or standing, he
had heard such words.[25]

Yet this same Irenaeus describes Clement as follows:

It might be said that he still heard the echoes of
the preaching of the Apostles, and had their
traditions before his eyes. And not only he, for
there were many still remaining who had been
instructed by the Apostles.[26]

Indeed, Irenaeus himself insists that his doctrine of the Sacrifice of the Mass is exactly what the apostles taught both Clement and Polycarp and all the rest of their converts. He writes:

Sacrifice as such has not been reprobated.
There were sacrifices then, sacrifices among
the people, and there are sacrifices now, sacrifices in the Church.[27]

In short, *Irenaeus sees no conflict at all between Clement's
teaching and that of the apostles.* Moreover, he seems to think
nobody who had been instructed by the apostles had any problem with Clement. This raised a colossal difficulty for my Pagan Creep theory. I had to believe Clement got away with this
supposed outrageous perversion of the Faith *while the entire
generation that had heard the apostles and endured the persecution of Nero said nothing about it.* I had to believe that Clement foisted "pagan gunk" on platoons of courageous believers
who were willing to suffer horrific deaths for the purity of their
faith, but who were either too fearful to point out or too stupid

to notice that he was adding wildly alien doctrines repugnant to the apostles.

The Pagan Creep theory was getting more difficult all the time. My reasoning now demanded four schizophrenic absurdities:

- That these presumably apostate successors were both promulgating alien pagan dogmas in direct defiance of the apostolic teaching *and* simultaneously undergoing suffering, persecution, and fearful deaths with an avowed determination to bear witness to the Faith of the apostles;
- That, in the case of Clement of Rome, the Apostle John was willing to drowsily ignore it while the Church at Corinth carefully preserved and circulated Clement's ideas about the supposedly unheard-of Sacrifice of the Mass;
- That not one single Christian anywhere else was willing to oppose this supposed gross heresy, even though they had heard the apostles with their own ears and were willing to die for what they had heard;
- And that while all this was going on, all these supposed heretics and lax stooges of paganism (whose secret desire was the subversion of Scripture) were all still willing to vehemently defend Scripture against the paganizing attacks of heretics like Marcion.

This seemed like a nest of contradictions. Nor did it get better when I looked at the case of yet another apostolic successor whom I had deemed quasi-pagan: Ignatius of Antioch (d. 110).

Writing a mere twenty years after the death of the Apostle John, Ignatius states plainly what I then took to be a quintessentially quasi-pagan piece of dogma: that "the Eucharist is the Flesh of our Savior Jesus Christ, Flesh which suffered for our sins and which the Father, in his goodness, raised up again."[28] Yet the very letter in which he records this teaching (and describes belief in it as a crucial litmus test for fidelity to the apostles) is composed while he is being conveyed to his death under Roman guard. His crime: refusal to renounce Jesus Christ and compromise his faith with paganism in any way.

Not long after, Ignatius was torn limb from limb by wild beasts, having written one of the most poignantly beautiful lines ever penned by a martyr for Jesus: "I am God's wheat, and I am to be ground by the teeth of wild beasts, so that I may become the pure bread of Christ."[29]

I was confronted yet again with the odd spectacle of a courageous disciple laying down his life for Christ and the purity of the Faith, yet a disciple who seemed devoted to a supposed quasi-pagan Catholic belief. Indeed, for Ignatius it is his devotion to the apostolic teaching that both ensures his martyrdom and compels him to write his letters to the churches on his journey to Rome. He writes precisely in order to urge the churches to stand guard against false teaching and to "take note of those who hold heterodox opinions on the grace of Jesus Christ."[30]

I asked myself hard questions. Was this really the way a crypto-pagan would talk or act? Would a martyr who insisted that "corrupters of families will not inherit the Kingdom of God"[31] corrupt the family of Christ with pagan notions about the Eucharist unknown to the apostles? Was it sensible to think that Ignatius would insist on utterly novel doctrines while simultaneously warning his flock not to be "led astray by other doctrines nor by old fables which are worthless"?[32] Was it even remotely likely that such a man would thereafter go to his death, first inventing the fiction of the Eucharist as True Body and Blood and then insisting that "if a man corrupt by evil teaching the faith of God, for the sake of which Jesus Christ was crucified, [that man has become so foul he will] depart into unquenchable fire; and so also will anyone who listens to him"?[33] And was it likely that seven churches who had heard the apostles with their own ears and who themselves had endured fire and sword for the Faith would embrace pagan notions without making a sound?

Obviously not. Yet my Pagan Creep theory demanded precisely this.

It also demanded that identical errors had to have crept into the Church repeatedly and in times and locations very distant from Ignatius and the other writers we have considered. The theory had to account not only for Ignatius', Polycarp's, and Clement's "paganization" of the Faith, but for the fact that everybody *else* seems to have been under the impression that the apostles taught these "errors" too — even though they are separated from these Fathers by many years and many miles.

Thus we find, for example, corroboration of Ignatius' understanding of Eucharist in Justin Martyr[34] (Rome, c. 150), Irenaeus[35] (Lyons, c. 180), and Athanasius[36] (Alexandria, c. 373). Yet none of these men tolerated paganism; all of them were willing to endure persecution, exile, and (in Justin's case) death for their devotion to Christ. They shared not only Ignatius' faith in the Real Presence, but Clement's conviction that the Eucharist is a true sacrifice (in fact, a participation in Christ's sacrifice) and Polycarp's teachings concerning Mary. In fact, Tertullian, Cyprian of Carthage, Cyril of Jerusalem, Gregory of Nazianzus, Gregory of Nyssa, John Chrysostom, Ambrose of Milan, Augustine of Hippo, Cyril of Alexandria, Theodoret of Cyr, Fulgence of Ruspe, and John of Damascus (to name just a few more witnesses from the second to the eighth centuries) all concur that these beliefs are in fact part of the *paradosis* handed down to the whole Church by the apostles and continuously believed everywhere and by all.

It was beginning to look as though there was a very good reason these and many other Catholic beliefs had "crept into" the Church so rapidly after John died: they had crept in via the apostles themselves and been preserved in the Church's tradition.

So I returned to the question with which we began this chapter: is the Catholic Church's reliance on tradition as circular as the Evangelical claim of self-attesting Scripture?

I thought of the line of apostolic successors, already traceable in the New Testament and abundantly attested by the immediate successors of the apostles, and reaching right down to our own day in the bishops of the Catholic churches.

I thought of the way in which this apostolic lineage had preserved, not only Scripture, but what looked for all the world like the thing Catholics call Sacred Tradition.

I thought of how it never seemed to occur to any of these ancient Christians that the Bible alone was the sole source of revelation.

I thought of the way in which these zealous arch-conservative purists and martyrs never regarded this extra-biblical Tradition as anti-biblical.

I thought of the way in which even we Evangelicals relied on this extra-biblical Tradition when it came to abortion, polygamy, the Trinity, the closure of public revelation, and the canon itself.

As I did this, it became harder and harder to see the circularity of the Catholic position. On the contrary, it was beginning to look a great deal as though there *was* a line pointing directly back to the apostles and through them to Christ.

Yet there *did* suddenly appear one circle which had hitherto eluded me. As I discovered this flood of evidence for an extra-biblical *paradosis* containing not only the basis for the New Testament canon, but all these Catholic beliefs as well, my increasingly lame theory of Immediate Apostasy by the Entire Church Before the Death of John began to sound uncomfortably familiar. For by a strange paradox, I realized that my Evangelical insistence on the Bible alone had brought me full circle in a way I had never anticipated. It was now *I* who was talking like a modernist.

Notes

1. Second Vatican Council, *Dogmatic Constitution on Divine Revelation*, 7, 2.
2. Thus, Acts 14:23 tells us that "Paul and Barnabas appointed elders for them in each church and, with prayer and fasting, committed them to the Lord, in whom they had put their trust." Likewise, Peter speaks to the elders of the churches,

not as though they have no authority, but as though they share his authority as "fellow elders" (1 Pt 5:1).

3. That is, Gnostics.

4. Irenaeus, *Adversus Haereses*, 3, 3, 1.

5. Irenaeus, *Adversus Haereses*, 3, 3, 3.

6. Clement, *Letter to the Corinthians*, 42, 1-4.

7. Clement, *Letter to the Corinthians*, 44, 1-3.

8. Ignatius, *Letter to the Smyrnaeans*, 8, 1.

9. Clement, *Letter to the Corinthians*, 40, 2; 44, 4.

10. Ignatius, *Letter to the Smyrnaeans*, 7, 1.

11. Tertullian, *Against Marcion*, 4, 40, 3.

12. Irenaeus, *Adversus Haereses*, 3, 1, 1.

13. A fact abundantly in evidence when one reads Evangelical apologetics à la Josh McDowell's *Evidence That Demands a Verdict*.

14. Papias, quoted in Eusebius's *History of the Church*, 3, 39, 15.

15. Justin Martyr, *Dialogue with Trypho the Jew,* 100.

16. Irenaeus, *Adversus Haereses*, 4, 26, 2.

17. Irenaeus, *Adversus Haereses*, 3, 3, 4.

18. Irenaeus, *On Sole Sovereignty*, quoted in Eusebius's *History of the Church*, 5, 20, 4.

19. Irenaeus, *On Sole Sovereignty*, 5, 20, 5-6.

20. Irenaeus, *Adversus Haereses*, 3, 3, 4.

21. *Martyrdom of Polycarp*, 9, 3.

22. Irenaeus, *Adversus Haereses*, 3, 22, 4.

23. Irenaeus, *Adversus Haereses*, 3, 3, 3.

24. Clement, *Letter to the Corinthians*, 44, 4.

25. Irenaeus, *On Sole Sovereignty*, quoted in Eusebius's *History of the Church*, 5, 20, 7.

26. Irenaeus, *Adversus Haereses*, 3, 3, 3.

27. Irenaeus, *Adversus Haereses*, 4, 8, 2.

28. Ignatius, *Letter to the Smyrnaeans*, 7, 1.

29. Ignatius, *Letter to the Romans*, 4, 1.

30. Ignatius, *Letter to the Smyrnaeans*, 6, 2.

31. Ignatius, *Letter to the Ephesians*, 16, 1.

32. Ignatius, *Letter to the Magnesians*, 8, 1.

32. Ignatius, *Letter to the Ephesians*, 16, 2.

34. *First Apology*, 65: "For not as common bread nor common drink do we receive these; but since Jesus Christ our Savior was made incarnate by the word of God and had both flesh and blood for our salvation, so too, as we have been taught, the food which has been made into the Eucharist by the Eucharistic prayer set down by Him, and by the change of which our blood and flesh is nourished, is both the flesh and the blood of that incarnated Jesus."

35. *Adversus Haereses,* 5, 2, 2: "He has declared the cup, a part of creation, to be His own Blood, from which He causes our blood to flow; and the bread, a part of creation, He has established as His own Body, from which He gives increase to our bodies."

36. *Sermon to the Newly Baptized*: "So long as the prayers of supplication and entreaties have not been made, there is only bread and wine. But after the great and wonderful prayers have been completed, then the bread is become the Body, and the wine the Blood, of our Lord Jesus Christ."

CHAPTER NINE
DYING AND RISING

It was déjà vu all over again. — Yogi Berra

M e? A modernist? Compare the theories of modernism with the Pagan Creep theory.

Modernism, as we recall, would have us believe that the Misunderstood Sage of Nazareth was both a profoundly wise rabbi and the dumbest cluck in human history. It proposes that a deeply spiritual man who saw through human souls like glass was incapable of noticing that his chosen disciples were people not even moderately competent at remembering a handful of his words and deeds. It also asserts that this devout Jew's love of the one true God of Israel so inspired these witless witnesses with devotion to their Master that they ran off the instant he was dead to blaspheme all he held dear. Modernism asks us to swallow the notion that these paragons of stupidity remained as stupid as ever for the rest of their lives, yet nonetheless managed to construct a militant, well-organized, theologically-sophisticated community capable of disturbing the Roman peace within twenty years of its founding and noticeable enough to invite Neronian persecution within thirty years. This impressive church, says modernism, was set in motion by a Galilean enigma whose few garbled phrases the New Testament writers, in their intense devotion to his memory, cannot for the life of them remember or even paraphrase, much less understand.

But if it is preposterous to say the entire apostolic community could simultaneously be this stupid and this brilliant, this forgetful and this obsessed with tradition, this unimaginative and this capable of flamboyantly inflating a rabbi whom even *they* couldn't remember into the Incarnate God of Israel, then how much *more* preposterous was my Pagan Creep theory? For it demanded I believe exactly the same thing of the apostles and *their* disciples. Indeed, it demanded the apostles had to have been twelve times more grotesquely incompetent than the already fabulously incompetent Jesus of modernism. It meant believing that everywhere the apostles went they — all of them — appointed successors who perverted their teaching on a dozen subjects as badly as modernism said the apostles had perverted Christ's. It meant that for sixty years of blood, sweat, and toil, the apostles made thousands of disciples so stupid that they could not grasp the most elementary teachings of their faith. It meant believing that their churches — all of them in north, south, east, and west — paganized Christianity (and paganized it everywhere in the same way) the instant the apostles died. It meant believing that these churches, together with their overseers who had been handpicked by the apostles, were constantly engaged in a schizophrenic campaign of deliberate pagan perversion of the Faith while simultaneously dying in droves for the purity of that Faith. It meant believing that the immediate successors to the apostles (and the flocks they shepherded) were both martyrs against all pagan compromise and punctilious preservers of Scripture, and yet simultaneously secret devotees of Mithra, Isis, and the mystery cults. It meant believing that in some fantastic fashion quite unparalleled in history, this outburst of amnesia, heresy, and schizophrenia (beginning well before the death of the Apostle John and spanning the length and breadth of the Roman Empire) managed to completely pervert the Faith once given to the saints without *one* of those saints taking any notice at all — the very same saints who were willing to be burned alive for Christ rather than offer a tiny pinch of incense to Caesar.

Seeing this brought me full circle to my final ironic realization: what had made me a sitting duck for modernism's attack on Scripture was nothing other than my well-meaning and thoroughly Evangelical rejection of Sacred Tradition. For I at last saw that modernism based its deepest assumptions, not on that Tradition, but on the *rejection* of it.

I had assumed that a tradition attested in the second or third century, yet not mentioned in Scripture, must surely be a human tradition. In discussions of the Eucharist, Purgatory, or Mary, I had simply brushed off Catholic references to the belief and practice of the bishops following the apostles. If it wasn't in Scripture, it was simply inadmissible evidence. Modernism merely took this attitude to its logical conclusion, arguing that the tradition of the canon (which is also only attested by bishops in the centuries following the apostles) was therefore just as unreliable as all the other aspects of the Sacred Tradition I rejected.

But modernism's case against the canon of Scripture made sense only *if* I continued in the assumption that all extra-biblical tradition was unreliable human tradition. If such a belief died in me (and what I had discovered about Scripture, history, Evangelical practice, Catholic theology, and commonsense had pretty well crucified it), then it was a whole new ball game. For if there *was* such a thing as a living Tradition of God handed down in both word and letter and preserved by the Church — as was now obvious — then my Bible-only view of revelation was as dead as the absurd Jesus of modernism. Indeed, they were buried in the same grave.

But buried, like the wheat seed, only for resurrection. For the nail that crucified my Bible-only belief was the very nail that was at last hammered firmly into "the church of the living God, the pillar and foundation of the truth" (1 Tm 3:15). And on that nail now hung all the truth and sanity of the gospel. In concluding that the Catholic picture of Sacred Tradition was far more believable than either modernism's picture of the Church after Christ or my Evangelical picture of the Church after the apostles, I found I had indeed lost something for Christ's sake only to get it back again. My safe and familiar Evangelical rejection of Sacred Tradition was dead. But also dead was my confusion about the canon and my need to seek after some ephemeral glow in my spirit or to eke out some arcane exegesis in order to know whether Ecclesiastes was inspired.

Instead, I could begin much closer to ordinary commonsense by asking the simple question, "Does the early Church look like an honest and intelligent bunch?" If the evidence is good that they are (and the evidence *is* good), then the evidence is equally good that the apostolic tradition they preserved and developed (including the Tradition of the Table of Contents) is trustworthy. If the evidence of *that* tradition is good, then the apostles who are the source of that tradition were also good and honest. If this is so, then the evidence for the deity of the Christ whom they proclaim is good. If that Christ is indeed the Son of God and has indeed promised to guide his Church into all truth and remain with it forever, then we can trust he will do just that.

Indeed, we can trust that the early Church itself did not need to rely on mysterious warm fuzzies to have this guidance either. Rather, all it needed was what it had: a living Body of Christ in union with apostolic successors who, by the gift of the Holy Spirit promised to the Church, preserved the common memory of the apostolic Sacred Tradition in both word and letter. By this Tradition, they slowly and painstakingly discerned which of the books in their library of early Christian writings were inspired and authoritative.

"But," someone might ask, "doesn't this slow process of discernment *refute* Sacred Tradition? After all, if it's so reliable, why did these early Christians have such a blurry picture of God's word? What sort of Christians were these early believers, not to have a clear understanding of what books were in their Bibles?"

Answer: they were great Christians, many of them heroes and martyrs for Christ, as we have seen. And a large part of their greatness lay in the fact that their understanding of God's word *was* quite clear; it was, for them, nothing more nor less than the apostolic *paradosis* in both word and letter guarded by apostolic successors like Timothy and Polycarp (which is to say, guarded by the Body of Christ). Believing this, they had confidence in the Body's Head that all challenges and obstacles to that *paradosis* would simply work "for the good for those who love him" (Rom 8:28) and that the saints would therefore "grow up into him who is the Head, that is Christ" (Eph 4:15).

However, they trusted this not because God had first given them a typewritten Table of Contents of Scripture in 95 A.D., but because "It was he who gave some to be apostles, some to be prophets, some to be evangelists, and some to be pastors and teachers, to prepare God's people for works of service, so that the body of Christ may be built up until we all reach unity in the faith and become mature, attaining to the whole measure of the fullness of Christ" (Eph 4:11-13). Therefore they trusted that the Holy Spirit would, as Jesus said, guide his Body — as a Body — into all truth (Jn 16:13) by the *paradosis* preserved by the apostolic successors (that is, the "pastors and teachers" given them by God). Should a Marcion or a Jesus Seminar create confusion about what parts of its written *paradosis* could be trusted, the apostles' successors would teach truly. The Body, receiving its daily bread, would be strengthened when the need arose and would, like Christ himself, grow in wisdom and stature (Lk 2:52). A canon of Scripture, rooted in Tradition, would develop under the guidance of the Spirit-led bishops, together with the rest of the Body, just as the boy Jesus developed a beard: when the time was ripe.

This explained something which had previously made little sense: namely, why the Catholic Church both staunchly insisted it could admit no new public revelation (as distinct from Mormonism) and yet just as staunchly insisted that its Tradition "developed." Hitherto, I had thought this way of talking about Tradition was bafflegab for justifying compromise with paganism and the invention of unbiblical beliefs. Yet as I looked at the New Testament period and the extremely uncompromising years following it, I thought that G.K. Chesterton had hit the target when he wrote:

> The critics of Catholic theology seem to suppose that it is not so much an evolution as an evasion; that it is at best an adaptation. They fancy that its very success is the success of surrender. But that is not the natural meaning of the word Development. When we talk of a child being well-developed, we mean that he has grown bigger and stronger with his own strength; not that he is padded with borrowed pillows or walks on stilts to make him look taller. When we say that a puppy develops into a dog, we do not mean that his growth is a gradual compromise with a cat; we mean that he becomes more doggy and not less.[1]

I was now persuaded that the New Testament and the post-apostolic period offers a picture of the Dog of Sacred Tradition flatly refusing any compromise with the Cat of Paganism — becoming "more doggy and not less." Thus, we see a community that can only be described as "arch-conservative" aiming to cling like barnacles to what the apostles said and taught. That is why Polycarp, Ignatius, and many others were martyred. That is why Irenaeus writes books like *Adversus Haereses* repudiating all fashionable Gnostic upgrades on the Faith once for all entrusted to the saints. For them as much as for the present-day Catholic Church, the *paradosis* is indeed complete. There will be no new "improvements" à la Joseph Smith, no "further revelations" from some angel telling us that, on second thought, there *is* more than one God. On the contrary, the Church has been given all it needs in the *paradosis* that was complete with the death of the Apostle

John. The bishop's only job now is, as the New Testament commands, to guard that *paradosis* by preserving the message, whether written or unwritten, without addition or deletion. It is the very model of conservatism.

Yet it is a living conservatism — a living faith of the dead rather than a dead faith of the living. The fully *formed* Puppy of Tradition is not fully *grown* either in the middle of the first century nor even at the end of the twentieth. Thus, as the Judaizers, Marcion, and Arius clearly demonstrated, new situations would sometimes demand that the Church make explicit some aspect of the *paradosis* which had hitherto been only implicit. How? By appealing, not to the Bible alone, but to the Bible in union with the Body of Christ, led by apostolic successors who were given authority, in Paul's words, to "command certain men not to teach false doctrines" (1 Tm 1:3).

So it is that in our own day, for example, the Church makes statements on the evils of physician-assisted suicide even though the New Testament has nothing to say on the matter. Yet nobody in his five senses claims that the present Church "invented" opposition to euthanasia from thin air. We all understand that the Church, by the very nature of its Tradition, has been opposed to physician-assisted suicide for two thousand years, whether or not anyone happened to be proposing it. It merely took the folly of the modern euthanasia movement to cause the Church to apply its Tradition to this concrete situation — and declare what it has always believed, even if it had never had to say it before.

Very well then, as with attacks on sacred human life in the twentieth century, so with attacks on Sacred Tradition in the previous nineteen. Jesus establishes the Tradition that he has not come to abolish the Law and the Prophets but to fulfill them (Mt 5:17). But when Tradition bumps into the theories of the circumcision party, the Council of Jerusalem is still necessary to authoritatively flesh that Tradition out. Moreover, the Council settles the question by calling the Bible, not to the judge's bench, but to the witness stand. Scripture bears witness to the call of the Gentiles, but the final judgment in Acts 15 depends on the authority of Christ speaking through his apostles and elders whose inspired declaration is not "The Bible says . . ." but "It seemed good to the Holy Spirit and to *us*. . . ." (Acts 15:28).

This is what links the Church in the apostolic age with the Catholic Church in the computer age. For this pattern of discernment and decision-making does not change in the years following the apostles. The Church after the apostles, staunchly conservative, settles huge questions ranging from the canon of Scripture to the nature of God and Christ in the same way it settled the circumcision issue at the Council of Jerusalem: with the Scripture in the witness stand and the Spirit-led Body of Christ on the judge's bench discerning the meaning of the Tradition more deeply.

Thus Tradition, both written and unwritten, contains the scattered seeds of the dogma of the Trinity. But the Council of Nicaea is still necessary to fully formulate that tradition when Arius challenges it. Tradition has always held that Christ is both God and man, but still the Church had to spell out what that means (at the Council of Ephesus, for example) when various challenges arise which assert his deity at the expense of his humanity and vice versa.

In all this, the Church, as ever, inseparably unites Scripture as the light and Sacred Tradition as the lens through which it is focused. In this way the mustard seed of the Kingdom continues to grow in that light, getting more mustardy, not less.

How then did Tradition develop with respect to the canon?

In some cases, as Papias, Irenaeus, Justin Martyr, and Eusebius show us, the Church in both East and West has a clear memory of just who wrote a given book and can remind the faithful of this when a Marcion tries to take away from the Tradition of Scripture by deleting Matthew, Mark, and John. In other words, there is, we might say, a Standard of Roots (based on Sacred Tradition) by which the Church weighs her canon. Likewise, when a Gnostic tries to add the Gospel of Thomas to the Church's written Tradition, the Church can point to the fact that, whatever the name on the label says, the contents do not square with the *paradosis* of the Church, so it must be a fake. In other words, there is also a Standard of Fruits. It is this dual standard of Roots and Fruits by which the Church discerns the canon — a dual standard which is wholly based on Sacred Tradition. The Church said, in essence, "Does the book have a widespread and ancient tradition concerning its apostolic origin? Check. Does the book square with the total *paradosis* we all learned from the apostles and the bishops they gave us? Check. Then it is to be used in public worship and is to be regarded as the word of God."

It was on *this* basis the early Church also vetoed Marcion's rejection of the Old Testament and accepted books ranging from Ecclesiastes, Esther, and the Song of Songs to the deuterocanonical books. For the churches founded by the apostles could trace the use of the Septuagint version of the Old Testament in public worship (which includes all these books) back to their remotest origins.[2] Therefore, the Body of Christ living after the apostles retained the apostles' practice of using the Septuagint (and therefore the deuterocanon) on the thoroughly traditional grounds, "If it's good enough for them, it's good enough for us."

This is not, of course, to imply that the Old Testament deuterocanon met with uncritical acceptance by one and all in the second, third, and fourth centuries any more than certain New Testament books like James, Hebrews, 2 Peter, or Revelation did. The Christian community had, after all, continued to rub shoulders with the Jewish community in the centuries after the apostles and, among other things, was confronted with the problem posed by the Jewish adoption (somewhere toward the end of the first century) of a shorter Old Testament which did not include the deuterocanon. Jerome, among a few other Fathers, was influenced by the Jewish community and thought the Church should adopt this shorter canon (which is what Protestants recognize today) rather than the Septuagint canon which constitutes the Catholic Old Testament. That is, he was somewhat dubious of the deuterocanonical books because he doubted their Roots in Old Testament Judaism, though not their Fruits or congruence with sound apostolic teaching. Similarly, as we shall see more fully in a moment, other local canons of Scripture were adopted by various communities under various bishops which sometimes excluded New Testament books now defined as canonical (such as 2 Peter) and included books now excluded (such as the Didache). Some of my Evangelical friends are tempted to read into this fuzzy process of discernment a collapse of the Catholic claim of infallibility. If the Church is infallible, they ask, why all the contradictory early canons? However, this is to overlook several things:

First, the fuzziness of the early Church concerning the canon is in fact damaging, not to the Catholic claim of infallibility, but to the notion of a self-attesting Bible. After all, if inspired Scripture is so obvious, why was it not obvious to the various communities around the Mediterranean? From a Catholic perspective, there is no particular mystery: the Church was very carefully weighing the various books by the Roots and Fruits standards and showing great caution, but it was not as yet claiming for any of these various early canons an infallible, universally held status. Irenaeus' canon, the Muratorian canon, Athanasius' 39th Festal Letter, and various other such lists of slightly varying "recognized books" were local decisions made by local councils and bishops and intended as directives, not for the whole Church, but for the particular sector of the Church affected by that council or bishop until such time as another council or bishop decided to alter the discipline of that area. To be sure, such decisions did partake of the Church's general Tradition (i.e., everybody regarded certain core documents such as the Law, the Prophets, the four gospels, and the Pauline epistles as inspired), but these early canons were not claiming to define a universal, infallible rule of faith for the whole Church as, say, the Ecumenical Council of Nicaea was when it defined the dogma of the Trinity.

Which brings us back to the point made previously: namely that the Church, guided by Spirit-led Councils and with a somewhat fuzzy canon of Scripture, formulated and promulgated such dogmas *years before* the Tradition of the Table of Contents assumed its present shape (a shape which included the deuterocanon) at the Councils of Cathage and Hippo. That is, the Church here, as in the book of Acts, behaves as though the necessary tools for knowing and defining divine revelation are not simply in Scripture alone, but in the full *paradosis* living in the Church of which Scripture was but one fuzzily defined part. Indeed, the crucial thing to keep in mind when considering the Catholic account of the development of the canon is that the Church did not finally and infallibly define the canon for another *twelve hundred years* (at the Council of Trent in the mid-1500s). Until that time, it held the canon as a kind of "generally received" Sacred Tradition (a lot like Evangelicals still do), yet still regarded the final discernment of which books belong in Sacred Scripture as a matter not formally closed and therefore open to some legitimate debate. This fuzziness was precisely why Jerome and other Fathers could hold that the deuterocanon might be excluded and other Fathers and theologians could insist they be included. For the Church in Council and in union with the See of Peter had not yet spoken definitively, therefore the matter was still somewhat open (just as the matter of circumcision was still somewhat open before the Council of Jerusalem and the matter of the deity of the Son and the Spirit was still somewhat open before Nicaea).

Yet, paradoxically, in closing the debate and formally canonizing Scripture, Trent did not do anything *new* any more than Jerusalem or Nicaea did. For all the Council did was reconfirm the Tradition of the Table of Contents which had been reflected in the general practice of Christendom, formulated by the local Councils of Cathage and Hippo and endorsed by Pope Damasus I about twelve-hundred years before. Such practice had been rooted, not in what the Jewish community after the apostles did, but in what the apostles themselves did before the Jewish community closed its canon. For as we have seen, the apostles often used the Septuagint (which included the deuterocanon) and taught their churches to do so as well. Therefore, the early Church (which adhered to apostolic rather than rabbinic tradition) stuck with the apostolic

Tradition here as elsewhere, even when the Jewish community, after the death of the apostles, opted to exclude the books of the deuterocanon. Likewise Trent, repeating the logic of the arch-conservative early Church, said of the deuterocanon, "If it's good enough for the apostles, it's good enough for us." Thus, nothing was added to the canon at Trent. Rather, the deuterocanon (and James and 2 Peter and Revelation, among others) were saved from *subtraction.*

This theological conservatism on the part of the Church also accounts for why the pagan poets quoted in the New Testament were never considered Scripture by the post-apostolic Church. For quite simply, none of the early churches had any apostolic tradition handed down concerning the use of, say, the works of Epimenides, therefore they did not regard his works as Scripture, though Paul quotes him. Again, it was by their Roots and Fruits that the Church's books were judged, and it was by the standard of Sacred Tradition that these Roots and Fruits were known.

These Root and Fruit standards are also clearly at work in the New Testament, especially in the case of Hebrews. As we have just noted, there was a certain amount of controversy in the early Church over the canonicity of this and other New Testament books. Some Fathers, especially in the West, rejected Hebrews (in no small part because of its lack of a signature). Yet the Church eventually accepted it. On what basis? Not on the basis that "it just felt right." On the contrary, it was judged apostolic because, in the end, the Church again discerned that it met the Roots and Fruits measure when stacked up against Sacred Tradition.

The Body of Christ had long believed that Hebrews said the same thing as the Church's Sacred Tradition handed down by the bishops. Thus, even Fathers (like Irenaeus) who rejected it from their canon of inspired Scripture still regarded it as a good book. That is, like the deuterocanon it had always met the Fruits standard. How then did it meet the Roots standard? In a nutshell, despite the lack of attestation in the text of Hebrews itself, there was an ancient tradition in the Church (beginning in the East, where the book was apparently first sent) that the book originated either from the pen of St. Paul or from one of his close associates such as Barnabas, Luke, or Apollos.[3] That tradition, which was at first better attested in the East than in the West (instantaneous mass communication being still some years in the future) accounts for the slowness of western Fathers (such as Irenaeus) to accept the book. But the deep-rootedness of the tradition of Pauline authorship in the East eventually persuaded the whole Church. In short, as with the question of circumcision in the book of Acts, the status of Hebrews was not immediately clear even to the honest and faithful (such as Irenaeus). However, the Church in council, trusting in the guidance of Holy Spirit, eventually came to consensus and canonized the book on exactly the same basis that the Council of Jerusalem promulgated its authoritative decree: "It seemed good to the Holy Spirit and to *us*. . . " [italics added].

Conversely, those books which the Church did not canonize as part of the New Testament were rejected because, in the end, they did not meet both the Root and Fruit standards of the Church's Sacred Tradition. Books like the Didache or the Shepherd of Hermas, while meeting the Fruit standard (and therefore finding their way into early local canons), were at length not judged to meet the Root standard since their authors were not held to be close enough to the apostolic circle — a circle which was, in the end, drawn *very* narrowly by the Spirit-led Church and which therefore excluded even Clement, since he, being "in the third place from the Apostles,"[4] was not as close to the apostles as Mark and Luke (who were regarded as recording the very gospels of Peter and Paul, respectively). This also explains why the writing of others who knew the apostles (such as Ignatius and Polycarp), were revered, yet excluded from the canon. The Church, arch-conservative as ever, relied on Sacred Tradition, not to keep adding to the New Testament revelation but to keep it as lean and close to the apostles as possible. This, of course, is why books which met neither the

Root nor Fruit standards of Sacred Tradition, such as the Gospel of Thomas, were rejected by the Church without hesitation as completely spurious.

In summary then, the early Church did not canonize books because they were self-attesting; they canonized books because they were attested by apostolic tradition. The books we have in our Bibles (and the ones we don't) were accepted or rejected according to whether they did or did not measure up to standards which were based entirely on Sacred Tradition and the divinely delegated authority of the Body of Christ.

But to say that was to say . . . what?

I thought back to the discoveries chronicled up till now. I thought of the way in which the Chosen People of both the Old Israel and the New preceded their Scriptures. I thought of the way in which the Church in Acts revered the Scriptures as the word of God and yet still located supreme decision-making authority, not in the Bible, but in the apostolic Church in union with the total *paradosis*, both written and unwritten. I thought of the way in which it never occurred to the post-apostolic mind to imagine that the Body of Christ and its Scripture could ever be truly opposed. I thought of how the successors to the apostles, so far from speaking of the Body as a "mere human community," instead seemed to take a dizzyingly high view not only of its written and unwritten Sacred Tradition, but of the Body itself.

As I thought of all these things, a passage from Augustine of Hippo I had stumbled on seemed to sum up the attitude, not only of these early Christians who guarded and canonized the Bible, but of at least one amazed twentieth century Evangelical: "I would not believe in the Gospel myself if the authority of the Catholic Church did not influence me to do so."[5]

Strong words indeed! Yet what were they but a plain restatement of the very thing I had taken so long to discover? Did Augustine disagree with Scripture in uttering such words? Was he not simply rephrasing Paul's own words to Timothy (words which preface 2 Timothy 3:16, the verse that I once looked to as proof of a self-attesting Bible)?

> But as for you, continue in what you have learned and have become convinced of, because you know those from whom you learned it, and how from infancy you have known the holy Scriptures, which are able to make you wise for salvation through faith in Christ Jesus (2 Tm 3:14-15).

For Paul, as for Augustine, "what you have learned and believed" (that is, the apostolic *paradosis*, both written and unwritten) is to be trusted, not because the Bible is self-attesting, but "because you know those from whom you learned it" — that is, the Body of Christ. Nor was this the only Pauline testimony to the authority of the Body of Christ. For every reading of the Bible made me more acutely aware that *many* verses treat that Body and its extra-biblical Tradition as though they exist in an indivisible and living union with the written word. Indeed, so far from my characterization of the Church as a "mere human community," I found the New Testament descriptions tended to speak far more often of the Church as "the fullness of him who fills everything in every way" (Eph 1:23) and to refer the authority of the Spirit-breathed book to the authority of the Spirit-filled Body.

Thus, for Paul, the inspired Scriptures are trustworthy, not because they attest to themselves, but because they rest on " the church of the living God, the pillar and foundation of the truth" (1 Tm 3:15), an inspired foundation made, not of paper and ink, but of "apostles and prophets, with Christ Jesus himself as the chief cornerstone" (Eph 2:20). In other words, the books are truthful because the Body which wrote, edited and canonized the books is the Body of Him who is Truth. That is why Paul declares that "through the Church," (and therefore through the Church's Bible as well) "the manifold wisdom of God should be made known" (Eph 3:10). And that is why the people who actually heard the apostles and their handpicked successors with their own ears act exactly like people under the impression that the pillar and foundation of their faith is not first and foremost a sheet of papyrus, but a living community which is "a letter from Christ . . . written not with ink but with the Spirit of the living God, not on tablets of stone but on tablets of human hearts" (2 Cor 3:2-3). As C.S. Lewis says:

> Nothing could be more unhistorical than to pick out selected sayings of Christ from the gospels and to regard those as the datum and the rest of the New Testament as a construction upon it. The first fact in the history of Christendom is a number of people who say they have seen the Resurrection. If they had died without making anyone else believe this "gospel" no gospels would ever have been written.[6]

In short, the New Testament believers did not come to trust the Body and its Head through the book; they came to the trust the book through the Body and its Head. They did so because, as the New Testament itself stresses again and again, that Body is every bit the inspired creation of God the Scriptures are (Mt 16:18). For it was on the Body as well as the Scripture that God breathed and said, "Receive the Holy Spirit" (Jn 20:22; 2 Tm 3:16). Both are the work of the Spirit who would lead the Body into all truth, as Christ promised. But the Body comes first; then, through it and in union with it, comes the written portion of its Sacred Tradition. Small wonder then if the students of the apostles demonstrate the universal conviction that the word of God resides not merely in Scripture but in the entire apostolic *paradosis* that is the lifeblood of that Body. For them, as for John, the Word is not merely made word. It is made flesh and dwells not merely in books and doctrines, but in the very being of the Body. Therefore, just as its Head is the Word made Flesh, so the Body is to make its Sacred Tradition not only words but flesh as well.

That is why John tells his flock, "Dear children, let us not love with words or tongue but with actions and in truth" (1 Jn 3:18). Similarly, this is why James says, "Do not merely listen to the word, and so deceive yourselves. Do what it says" (Jas 1:22). Likewise, Paul insists that if I can "fathom all mysteries and all knowledge, and if I have a faith that can move mountains, but have not love, I am nothing" (1 Cor 13:2). For John, James, and Paul — as for their Master — the Word must be *enfleshed* if it is to be fully real.

For the same reason Paul also sees no problem with the Word being enfleshed if it is to be fully *communicated*. Thus, he tells the Corinthians that one of the loudest testimonies they offer to the cross of Christ is not verbal, but bodily: "For whenever you eat this bread and drink this cup, you proclaim the Lord's death until he comes" (1 Cor 11:26). Likewise, he insists that we die with Christ, not merely through a verbal profession of faith (though there is provision for this in rare and extreme cases such as the Good Thief) but "through baptism" (Rom 6:4). And in the same way, James teaches that the elders should offer prayers, not only with their minds and hearts, but with the oil of anointing as well (Jas 5:14). In other words, it began to look as though the *paradosis* is not delivered merely in what the Body says or writes, for bodies don't merely *say* things; they *do* things too. And what the Body did began to look as though it involved not only morals and ethics but what Catholic teaching called "liturgy and sacraments."

Which meant that though I had *discovered* Sacred Tradition (if you can discover something the Catholic Church has known for two thousand years) I was only scratching the surface in *exploring* it. All the aspects of Sacred Tradition I had thus far painstakingly unearthed were merely a sort of doctrinal footprint left by the living Body in intimate union with the living Christ. Such footprints were indeed sure and certain marks of the Faith, but the Faith itself consisted, not merely in doctrinal pronouncements, or even in the Scriptures, inspired and inerrant though they be, but in *everything* the apostles handed on. "Everything," according to Catholic teaching, was "everything which contributes toward holiness of life and increase of faith of the people of God. Thus, the Church, in her doctrine, life and worship, perpetuates and hands on to all generations all that she herself is, all that she believes."[7]

"All that she is, all that she believes." In other words, Sacred Tradition lives not in the footprint, but in the Foot. For, according to Catholic teaching, the Tradition and the Body are one in a union that is expressed, not only in its documents and doctrines (that is, the whole lens of interpretive Tradition in union with the light of Scripture), but in the Body's whole being as well (that is, its sacraments, structure, liturgy, community, hierarchy, and way of life). Therefore the revelation of Christ, according to Catholic teaching, is likewise given, not merely in what the Body says but in what it *is* and what it *does*. Thus I had yet to find out about Sacred Tradition as it is encompassed and expressed in:

- The sacramental life of the Church — how, by whom, and to whom the sacraments are administered, what they mean, and what they are;
- The liturgical and prayer life of the Church — how, when, and to whom the Church prays;
- The moral, ascetic, and mystical life of the Church;
- And the very structure of the Church herself.

We shall not explore these things in greater detail here, since to do so would turn this book into a full-blown *Catechism of the Catholic Church*, a work that has already been written by people with the competence to do it and one to which I now happily refer you if, like me, you find yourself persuaded of the sanity of Catholic Sacred Tradition and want to know more.

Of course, I know from experience that the Catholic view of Tradition still contains difficulties for many a believer, Evangelical and otherwise. Even after I had become convinced of the reality of Sacred Tradition, nonetheless Purgatory, Immaculate Conception, indulgences, and other such sharp spikes of Sacred Tradition still remained points for me to grapple with just as much as they remain for any other person serious about understanding the Catholic Faith. I had to grapple with them because, however tempting it was to take the "useful" portions of Catholic Tradition and run off with them to challenge modernism, I now knew we Evangelicals could no more do so than we could pick a favorite thread from Christ's robe and run off with it. For no part of Sacred Tradition, written or unwritten, can be set above (or below) the authority of the Church with which it is seamlessly woven together, or else the whole Tradition (and therefore the written Tradition which is the Bible — and therefore all Christianity) unravels. The authority of his Church, like Christ's robe, is seamless, woven in one piece from top to bottom.

This is not to say that all aspects of Catholic Tradition are equally important. The Church itself acknowledges the reality of the hierarchy of truth and is quite matter-of-fact in saying that some Tradition (such as the Trinity) is irreformable big "T" Tradition, while other tradition (for example, the Friday abstinence from meat or some other delectable) is small "t" tradition. The latter can be altered or even set aside by the Church and has been on occasion, for it is a mere discipline and not a cornerstone of what must be believed always, everywhere, and by all. But the big "T" stuff cannot be altered without striking at the very heart of the Faith.

Which left me (as it leaves you, good reader) with a challenge.[8] According to Catholic belief, the very doctrines which irk most Protestant believers (such as Purgatory, the Assumption of Mary, the Infallibility of the Pope, and so forth) are doctrines which cannot be set aside since they are squarely located under the big "T" heading by the Catholic Church and are therefore immovable features of Sacred Tradition — the very same Tradition which tells us what is and is not in our Bible and does so in a coherent voice of authority sounding down the centuries through a line of bishops leading inexorably back to Jesus Christ himself. In other words, I was obliged to either:

1. Find out if the *whole* Catholic Tradition was truly coherent; or,

2. Arbitrarily reject the bits I was uncomfortable with, but

simultaneously exploit Catholic Tradition's authority (where it was useful against modernism) — all the while hoping that both Evangelicals and modernists (not to mention the Holy Spirit) would not laugh at my wholesale inconsistency.

I chose the first route. In so doing I discovered (in a journey I will not recount here) that, in the final analysis, there is not a single solitary aspect of Catholic Sacred Tradition from the Immaculate Conception to the Eucharistic Real Presence to Purgatory to indulgences to prayers to the saints to the Papacy to Infallibility to the Assumption of Mary that is *anti*-biblical.

Are many of these doctrines partially extra-biblical? Yes, though all are rooted in Scripture as well. But, as we have seen, extra-biblical revelation is part of Evangelical belief just as it is of Catholic. Indeed, Evangelical extra-biblical revelation is, in every one of its big "T" manifestations, unconsciously borrowed from Catholic extra-biblical revelation. So I could hardly object to Catholic teaching on this basis. On the contrary, as I was now acutely aware, to show that these Catholic dogmas were un-Christian (as, for example, the modernist attack on the canon is certainly un-Christian), I would have to show that they both opposed Scripture and were without root in the apostolic *paradosis* preserved in the Church's Tradition (as modernism is). But with Catholic big "T" Tradition I never could show such a thing. In fact, it became harder and harder to see how the fullness of that *paradosis* (of which so many denominations unconsciously possessed fragments) was preserved anywhere else than in the one, holy, catholic, and apostolic Church in union with Peter and his successors.

Which is why, to make a long story short, I am now a "completed Evangelical." Compelled by the depth, sanity, and beauty of the Catholic Faith, I have pursued the Lord Jesus Christ into the heart of the Catholic communion. In the end, I found I gave up nothing of what my own native Evangelicalism has always affirmed; rather, I only gave up the things we had mistakenly denied. I found my little kernel of Bible-only wheat, once dead, put down roots as deep as the whole of Sacred Tradition and grew up under the towering sky of Catholic light into a Christian faith far stronger, greener, and more fruitful than ever before — and one more rooted in the inspired Scripture than it ever was. I found that my Evangelical love of the word of God grew stronger than ever when rooted in the rich soil of apostles, martyrs, saints, and doctors of the Church. Here, at last, it was safe from the depredations of wolves in tweed and turtlenecks.

I found all this because I found that the Catholic Faith loved Jesus Christ just as my native Evangelicalism did, insisting "Sacred Scripture is the speech of God as it is put down in writing under the breath of the Holy Spirit."[9] Yet the Church did so in a way that was rooted in the authority of God himself, an authority that did not pit the Body of Christ against its own inspired word or argue in a circle. It did so in a way which gently but firmly insisted on the reality that the revelation who is Christ remains with and in, not merely the Bible, but his *people* till the end of the age. It did so in a way which honored my own Evangelical tradition as a real, though incomplete, participation in Christ's Sacred Tradition, yet which also challenged me to come to complete unity with the whole of that Tradition. It did so in a way that showed how such fullness looked by fully receiving our Lord in the very ways that Sacred Scripture itself refers us to: in the living sacraments of the Church, the living teaching of the Magisterium, and the living fullness of one, holy, catholic, and apostolic Body in which dwell the "riches of his glorious inheritance" (Eph 1:18). For as both the Catholic Church and the authors of Scripture knew (and I so belatedly discovered), such an inheritance could not be contained in any book, however inspired. It was and is fully embodied, preserved and delivered to a hungry world only in the fullness of the Faith once for all entrusted to the saints.

Notes

1. G.K. Chesterton, *St. Thomas Aquinas: The Dumb Ox* (Garden City, N.Y.: Image Books, 1956), pp. 27-28.

2. In fact, many of the citations of Old Testament Scripture by the New Testament writers are, in fact, citations of the Septuagint (see, for example, Mk 7:6-7, Heb 10:5-7).

3. *The Jerome Biblical Commentary*, Vol. 2, Raymond E. Brown, S.S., Joseph A. Fitzmeyer, S.J., Roland E. Murphy, O. Carm., eds. (Englewood Cliffs: Prentice-Hall, 1968), p. 381.

4. Irenaeus, *Adversus Haereses*, 3, 3, 3.

5. Augustine, *Against the Letter of Mani*, 5, 6.

6. C.S. Lewis, *Miracles* (New York: MacMillan, 1947), p. 144.

7. Second Vatican Council, *Dogmatic Constitution on Divine Revelation*, 8, 1.

8. A challenge which, if you wish to take it up, can be pursued with the help of some of the handy materials offered in the appendix.

9. Second Vatican Council, *Dogmatic Constitution on Divine Revelation*, II, 9.

APPENDIX

The Catholic communion is a big place. Like all big places, it has a lot of people in it, saying a lot of things. This can lead to confusion both for the inquirer and for the lay Catholic who is trying to make heads or tails of what the Church teaches. We can often assume that anyone who says, "I'm Catholic!" therefore must *know* what the Church teaches. Yet merely being a member of the Catholic communion does not automatically mean that a person knows or even cares what the Church actually teaches (a fact abundantly demonstrated by the writings of John Dominic Crossan detailed elsewhere in this book). So whether you are someone who is looking at the Church for the first time or are a Catholic of fifty years who is wondering just what the Church says and why, accept no substitutes: get real Catholic teaching from informed and committed Catholic sources. Here are a few I think are useful:

Books

Catechism of the Catholic Church. It is now available in general bookstores in paperback for around $7.00. Parts of it may be a bit technical in vocabulary, but it is an authoritative summary of the official teaching of the Catholic Church. One note of caution, though: the *Catechism* is written more to tell you *what* the Church believes, not to give a blow-by-blow account of *how* she came to believe it. Thus, a reader curious about, say, Trinitarianism, will not find a detailed discussion of the Arian controversy. He will simply find an explication of the dogma of the Trinity which was formulated as a result of that controversy. Which is why I also suggest:

The Catholic Catechism by Father John Hardon, S.J. This splendid catechism is laid out in such a way as to show the roots of Catholic doctrine in both Scripture and Tradition and to trace the development of these doctrines over the centuries. Extremely useful!

Catholic and Christian: An Explanation of Commonly Misunderstood Catholic Beliefs by Alan Schreck. The author makes a special effort to explain Catholic beliefs in terms familiar to Evangelical Protestants, to show that while there are real differences between Catholics and Protestants, there also are more points of agreement than many people realize.

The Compact History of the Catholic Church by Alan Schreck. If you want to understand someone, you have to know where they've been. Here is a good book on where the Catholic Church has been.

Evangelical is Not Enough by Thomas Howard. A delightful book in felicitous prose that takes us further up and further into the sacramental and liturgical life of Catholic Christendom. Highly recommended.

Fundamentals of the Faith: Essays in Christian Apologetics by Peter Kreeft. This book is more than apologetics. After giving reasons for believing in God, believing in the deity of Jesus Christ, and believing in the authority of the Catholic Church because it was founded by Jesus Christ to teach in His name, Kreeft explains a lot of what general Christian and specifically Catholic beliefs mean for us.

A Map of Life; Theology for Beginners; Theology and Sanity; To Know Christ Jesus. All of these are by Frank Sheed. They were written primarily for Catholics to explain the meaning and richness of truths they already accepted. Therefore, there is no attempt to prove that the doctrines are true, just to show what they mean. *To Know Christ Jesus* is not so much doctrine as a discussion of the reality of Jesus as God incarnate.

Rome Sweet Home by Scott and Kimberly Hahn. A moving

account of the spiritual journey of this former Presbyterian pastor and his wife into full communion with the Catholic Church.

Surprised by Truth, edited by Patrick Madrid, is a lovely collection of personal testimonies by various people who have become Catholic.

This Is My Body: An Evangelical Discovers the Real Presence by Mark P. Shea. A small book which aims to explain the biblical basis for the Catholic understanding of the Eucharist. It is available from Christendom Press, 134 Christendom Dr., Front Royal , VA 22630 (telephone 540-636-2900).

And as a final book recommendation: just about anything by G.K. Chesterton is a good read. However, I would especially recommend the following (all available from Ignatius Press): *Orthodoxy*; *The Everlasting Man*; *St. Francis of Assisi*; *St. Thomas Aquinas: The Dumb Ox*; *The Catholic Church and Conversion*.

Periodicals

All the magazines published by Our Sunday Visitor, Inc., are good, including *Our Sunday Visitor*, *New Covenant*, *Catholic Heritage*, *Catholic Parent*, *The Pope Speaks* and, especially of interest to those curious about the Catholic communion: *The Catholic Answer*, a magazine devoted to teaching the Faith. All these magazines can be subscribed to by calling Our Sunday Visitor Publishers at 800-348-2440.

Also excellent is *Catholic Faith* magazine, published by Ignatius Press and dedicated to clearly teaching the doctrines of the Church. The magazine is $24.95 per year and you can subscribe by calling 800-651-1531 or by mailing *Catholic Faith*, PO Box 160, Snohomish, WA 98291-0160.

In a similar vein, there is *Catholic Dossier* magazine (also from Ignatius), which tackles a different area of the Church's teaching in-depth every issue. An extremely useful resource for getting past mere "surface thinking" and digging into the Church's tradition more deeply. The magazine is $24.95 per and you can subscribe by calling 800-651-1531 or by mailing *Catholic Dossier*, PO Box 1639, Snohomish, WA 98291-1639

Crisis is a good journal of lay Catholic opinion and debate about current issues. You can subscribe by writing the magazine at P.O. Box 495, Notre Dame, IN 46556 or by phoning them at 800-852-9962. The cost is $25.00 for eleven issues. It is also available on-line and can be subscribed to at http://www.catholic.net:80/RCC/Forms/CrisisSub.html.

New Oxford Review, 1069 Kains Ave., Berkeley, CA 94706. A fine magazine put out by ecumenically-minded, yet committedly-orthodox Catholics, many of them originally from a Protestant background. Subscription costs are $19.00 for one year, $35.00 for two years and $48.00 for three years.

This Rock, a good magazine of Catholic apologetics, is published by Catholic Answers, a good Catholic apologetics organization. Annual subscription rates: $24.00 to U.S. addresses; $30.00 (U.S. currency) to Canadian and Mexican addresses; $35.00 (U.S. currency) elsewhere. Requests for subscriptions should be sent to *This Rock*, P.O. Box 17490, San Diego, CA 92177.

Media Resources

Saint Joseph Communications, Inc., P.O. Box 720, West Covina, CA 91793 (telephone: 818-331-3549, or toll-free outside of California: 800-526-2151). St. Joseph's has numerous tapes by Scott Hahn, a first-rate teacher and theologian (and a former Presbyterian who knows in his bones the heartfelt concerns of Protestants looking at the Catholic communion and trying to make sense of it all). You couldn't ask for a better guide for the perplexed.

EWTN: The Eternal Word Television Network. If it's on your cable system, take a peek at the network Mother Angelica built. Many useful shows here if you are trying to find out what the Church teaches and why.

There are also many Catholic resources on-line including:
- The Catholic Information Center on Internet (http://www.catholic.net:80)

- Our Sunday Visitor Press (osv@catholic.net)
- Ignatius Press (http://www.ignatius.com)
- The Nazareth Resource Library created by James Akin (http://www.primenet.com/~jakin)
- The New Advent Catholic Website (http://www.knight.org/advent/index.html)
- Catholic Answers (http://www.electriciti.com/~answers).

Further Resource/Support Groups

The Association of Evangelical Catholics, c/o The Little Portion, Route 3, Box 608, Eureka Springs, AR 72632. This is an affiliation of "completed Evangelicals" who aim to offer support and spiritual aid to one another through sharing of ideas and resources.

Catholic Answers, P. O. Box 17490, San Diego, CA 92177 (telephone: 619-541-1131) is an organization dedicated to explaining practically any question you could possibly have about the Catholic communion. It carries a large selection of books and tapes from orthodox Catholic publishers.

Defending the Faith, Franciscan University at Steubenville, Steubenville, OH 43952 (telephone: 1-800-466-8336). This yearly conference is a chance to see on-fire Catholics in their natural habitat and ready to explain the Faith in wonderful and living color.

Family Life Center, 650 Gates Ave., Port Charlotte, FL 33952 (telephone: 813-743-7746). An organization dedicated to the renewal of the family, the Church, and our culture. Its president, Steve Wood, is an articulate exponent of the Catholic Tradition. He has many teachings and talks available on tape.

The Network, P.O. Box 4100, Steubenville, OH 43952 (telephone: 800-466-8336). This organization, headed by Marcus Grodi, is primarily aimed at providing ideas, resources and fellowship for former Protestant clergy who have entered the Catholic Church and are looking for places to "plug in" and put their considerable gifts to work.

INDEX